QUEERING
THE
RUNES

QUEERING
THE RUNES

Reclaiming Ancestral Wisdom
in Rune Magic & Mythology

SIRI VINCENT PLOUFF

foreword by LARA VESTA

WEISER
BOOKS

This edition first published in 2024 by Weiser Books, an imprint of
Red Wheel/Weiser, LLC
With offices at:
65 Parker Street, Suite 7
Newburyport, MA 01950
www.redwheelweiser.com

ISBN: 978-1-57863-837-6

Library of Congress Cataloging-in-Publication Data

Names: Plouff, Siri Vincent, 1988- author. Title: Queering the runes : reclaiming ancestral wisdom
in rune magic and mythology / Siri Vincent Plouff ; foreword by Lara Vesta.
Description: Newburyport, MA : Weiser Books, [2024] | Includes bibliographical references. |
Summary: "This book is a love letter to the runes, the gods, and the people who follow the Nordic
path. It also presents an alternative approach to the runes, offering a contemporary, inclusive,
nonbinary, and forward-thinking approach. The author gives the traditional meanings of the runes,
then helps the reader to 'queer' the runes in their own way, to get to know their energy, and to
use them move forward in a journey of self-discovery"-- Provided by publisher.
Identifiers: LCCN 2024034348 | ISBN 9781578638376 (trade paperback) |
ISBN 9781633413351 (ebook) Subjects: LCSH: Runes. | Fortune-telling by runes. |
Divination. | Mythology, Norse. | BISAC: BODY, MIND & SPIRIT / Divination / Runes |
BODY, MIND & SPIRIT / Occultism
Classification: LCC BF1891.R85 P56 2024 | DDC 133.3/3--dc23/eng/20240826
LC record available at https://lccn.loc.gov/2024034348

Cover and interior design by Sky Peck Design
Typeset in Aller

Printed in the United States of America
IBI
10 9 8 7 6 5 4 3 2 1

To my beloved parents, Lavonne and Joe.
You are like the earth, steady and strong.
You have guided me through life and provided an
abundant garden in which to grow.
This book is for you, our shared ørlog,
and a blessing to all of our ancestors.

Contents

Foreword

One of my favorite practices these days is to challenge my own fixed ideas. A question I like to ask is, "What if I'm wrong?" and then to see where the thought exercise leads.

In *Queering the Runes*, Siri Vincent Plouff invites all of us to ask, "What if I'm wrong?" From this place of inquiry we travel deep into the ancestral root culture of the runes. Plouff then bids us to set aside what we think we know, and begin again.

Our ancestors had strict social codes of honor and conduct that governed their lives and their relationships with the divine. These models are not something to toss aside. Just because we've been told the story of our history over and over we may think we know better. But we owe it to our ancestors to learn as much as we can about their lifeways, skills, crafts and traditions. Committing to ancestral spiritual connection means a lifetime of study, interpretation, and application. To truly honor our ancestral inheritance—as fragmented and disrupted as it may be— is an endless attempt, a surrender to all we cannot know, and a call to learning ever more.

Attempt does not mean we will always be right, know right, interpret right. Attempt allows for the failure—of ideas when new information is accessed, of gnosis when presented in community—and for change. We can change our minds, hearts, and perspectives when new information comes through.

This is a demonstratable ancestral attitude. All history shows the test of idea, ideology, practice, and perspective. We cannot rewrite history from a single point of view. To do so is to commit the same omissions and obfuscations that have doomed so much traditional ancestral knowledge.

Instead we may trust in the wisdom of our ancestors—who live in us—open to possibility, and rigorously test through research and practice the hypotheses of our era.

All history also shows what will endure with the passage of time. Our own time is no different. We will be tested too.

Much of the modern information about the runes is not based on their contemporary ancestral text sources—those are few—and the documentation we do have is often secondary or tertiary material, unreliable and reinterpreted. So there is a lot of room in rune study for new experiences and growth.

Empowering people to their own research and relationships has been the goal of my work, and I see this reflected in Siri's *Queering the Runes*. The opportunity for direct experience is here, along with an urging to find supportive community for vetting your gnosis.

As you read you may be pressed at the edges by new information, and when this happens I invite you to explore my second favorite thought exercise—a perfect complement to runic study. I call it "holding the both," and it simply means opening the mind and allowing disparate ideas to exist simultaneously before engaging them in the rigors of your own intellectual and spiritual challenging. We are often so quick to embrace, or dismiss, things outside our sphere of knowing or comfort. But opening to the possibility of the both-ness, that something can be both real and not real, masculine and feminine, true and not true, deconstructs any presumed binaries while preparing us for the trial of embodied spiritual experience—putting ideas into practice. *Queering the Runes* holds the both-ness of potential while honoring ancestral traditions, calling us into the wisdom of lived exploration.

By this and every effort may the balance be regained—ᚠᚱᚾ

—Lara

1

Introduction

Many years ago I was dragged—kicking and screaming—into working with Òðinn. I cast a circle, ready to rededicate myself after a difficult coven experience, calling out to any spirit who might want to work with me. I fully assumed that I would be working with a goddess, probably a Celtic or Hellenic one at that. I was prepared for her to come forward, but instead the Allfather came into my circle and introduced himself. He was wry, a twinkle in his eye, his wide hat pulled low, and a staff in hand. I asked what he wanted to be called, and he answered, "Odin."

Later, I scoffed. What are the odds that the Allfather wanted to work with me? I was just a lowly witch, initiated into Wicca and looking for something else, but not sure what. In spite of wanting to find a personal goddess, I wasn't even certain I believed in deities. The very concept of a creator god seemed impossible in my scientific mind. I told myself it was probably just a mischievous spirit who was also named Odin that I was working with (because I do have experience with many mischievous sprites). I was too intimidated by the idea that this was the High One, and so I eased into the relationship, eyes wide open and skeptical.

The truth of the matter is that I didn't want it to be a Norse god. I had always been bored by my mom's interest in Norwegian American culture. The *lefse* my grandmother made every Christmas did not taste special on my tongue. Along my path I had run into several less-than-kind Norse pagans, and by this point I had decided that Norse work was a red flag for me in my search for a community. Of the nasty experiences I had experienced in polytheist, poly-pantheon covens, the worst actors were the ones that followed the Norse gods. I didn't feel comfortable learning to read runes in my original coven, and honestly that was for the better because I would eventually part ways with them. So it was in my own best interests to convince myself that this wasn't *the* Odin—it was merely a spirit that called themselves Odin. This was not a mechanism of disbelief, it was a method of protecting my sense of safety within faith.

The first thing that helped me warm up to the Norse gods was the grand mythology. I was surprised by how fresh the *Prose* and *Poetic Edda* felt. It was easy to submerge myself in the stories of Loki, Thor, Odin, and Freyja, to feel these personalities come off the page. The drama of Ragnarök piqued my interest; I could personally relate to it as a sort of prophecy of impending climate catastrophe.

As a queer nonbinary femme, it is very important for me to look at my spirituality and see acceptance for who I am. Before I began working with the Norse pantheon, I shunned them. They were too masculine. The Vikings were infamous raiders who participated in the slave trade. That aspect of my own ancestry disgusted me. I had sought paganism as a place to escape the patriarchy, to dream of something bigger and better than capitalism. I wanted to return to my roots, but at the same time was unwilling to cast a critical eye at what those roots really meant. Why would I want that energy anywhere near me?

But this is just one part of the story.

The idea of the "Viking" is incredibly popular right now, and that has its ups and downs. Stories about Vikings are seeing a resurgence, in large part thanks to the TV show *Vikings*, as well as some elements of *Game of Thrones* that evoke Norse culture (cough the wildlings cough). The popular vision of the Viking is now an honor-bound tree of a man, who will fight fiercely and to the death. Vikings in this sense are brutal, primitive, and they seemed to me more like Conan the Barbarian than Merlin. There are a lot of stereotypes of the Old Norse as incredibly masculine marauders who pillaged around the world. But to go Viking was really only a small part of Nordic culture, for a limited period of time throughout a long and vast history. Most medieval Nordic people were farmers or lived in small agrarian communities otherwise supporting them. As with everything, the further away from stereotypes you get, the deeper into the truth of it you get.

It is because of these stereotypes that many people might be surprised at the fact that my work with the runes has been deeply healing, and especially healing in my own queerness and internal masculinity. I have a history of sexual assault and violence at the hands of men, to the point of being uncomfortable in a room with any man other than my father or boyfriend for much of my twenties. This made it very difficult to recognize the positive masculinity within myself, but that is a book for a different time. This fear of men was a large part of why I was so confused when I called in a goddess to work with me, and was visited instead by Odin. When Odin continued to show up throughout the next several months in my rituals, I knew that I needed to pay attention. There were too many synchronicities to ignore. A murder of crows taking up residence near my apartment, coming across Norse myth and legend as I was reading other works, my curiosity being piqued when my grandmother told a story about her family. This was not something I could ignore.

It was around this time that I also started to shed my identity as a Wiccan.

The runes chose me.

.It was an unusual choice—I'm not the kind of person you think of when you think of a Norse pagan. I am not obsessed with Vikings, or martial arts. I am not a man. I am not a white supremacist. Here's what I am: queer as hell, nonbinary, disabled, and a writer. And yet, I know that there are countless others that make up a growing, global kindred of heathens who share my values and some of my identities. Perhaps this is why the runes came to me when they did—because now is the time to expand beyond 20th-century views of Norse paganism.

This book is a love letter to the runes, the gods, and the people who follow the Nordic path. I want to present an alternative approach to the runes, one that creates a gentle container for those who want to follow this path. There are others who have started to forge this path before me, and to whom I am endlessly grateful. And yet—it still feels like something has been missing. A lot of the work that has been done to reclaim heathenry from white supremacy has focused on honoring the feminine within the tradition. This has been absolutely essential—as toxic masculinity is one of the first things that many outsiders think of when they think of Norse pagans. However, this femininity is so often presented as one side of a binary. Because of this, it often feels very heterocentric.

This book is the book I wanted when I started practicing Nordic paganism.

As a queer, leftist, environmentalist, nonbinary person, I don't see myself reflected in a lot of mainstream work on heathenry, which is strange considering how very queer so many of the deities and beings of Norse mythology are. There are so many transformative aspects of the mythology, and the culture that stems from that mythology, that the lack of queer representation in heathen writing feels strange, even absUrð.

When I began working with Odin and the runes, it was because they were just so present. There are only so many times the synchronicities come together before you have to listen. So, like Odin, I've gone a bit blind into my practice, and I've opened my eyes to heathenry and Nordic folk magic. I met Freyja, and Loki, and my own ancestors. The Minneapolis Nordic Women's Retreat and Völva Stav Guild really showed me what a healthy heathen community can look like: mutual respect, wisdom, laughter, and a deep commitment to creating communities of care.

Edda means great-grandmother.[1] The wisdom has been hidden there all along, underneath the layers of loud people who aren't actually engaging with the sources. I don't feel bashful anymore. And while it's important to continue to unravel white supremacy from heathenry, it's also important to understand that there is so much more here than to identify in opposition to something.

Once I embraced Odin and the runes as a major part of my path, I embarked on a healing journey that helped me ultimately come to terms with so much, including my nonbinary identity. It feels strange to think of these letters from a dead language as the catalyst for this

---

1   Liberman. "Ten Scandinavian and North English Etymologies."

decidedly modern path. The runes collapse time. It's actually helpful that they are letters from a dead language—because sometimes, to get over the clashing static of our own modern psyches, we need to look to something older. We need to slow down and interpret something that isn't directly of our own world.

This makes for a distinctly unique way of accessing our inner realms. I've always felt, when picking up a new method of divination, that it's like learning a new language. You learn how this specific tool works for you, the way that you have to slow down and open your mind to the messages. Runes are literally a language, avatars of meaning in and of themselves, and in their combinations. But it's time to begin to speak that language with a modern understanding. We go back in order to go forward.

The backbone of this book is inclusivity. I am working to write something that will make heathenry accessible to those who don't normally feel as welcome in this community. But of course, I'm using the word "Norse" to describe this practice. In a time when white supremacists are marching in the streets under the banner of runes, it's important to be clear about the tenets inclusive in Norse practice.

The heathenry that I practice is culturally specific, but it is also possible for anyone of any background to take up this practice. Heathenry is cultural because it relies on a specific set of shared cultural beliefs and practices—but perhaps even more than that, it is inspired by precious works of literature and myth.

At its core, heathenry is a reconstruction of the beliefs and practices of pre-Christian Germanic tribes. Different academic traditions define "Germanic" differently, but usually when I talk about the Germanic peoples I mean people who speak a Germanic language (German, Dutch, Danish, Norwegian, Swedish, and English, though people inhabiting present-day England, Scotland, Wales, and Ireland are generally not included in this ancient "Germanic Tribes" until the Saxons arrive).[2] Really, there were many, many local practices that these tribes engaged with, and there was a huge diversity in beliefs between different tribes.

---

2 "Germanic peoples," Wikipedia.

Their geographic region spanned Central Europe (modern-day Austria, Germany, Eastern France, Netherlands, Denmark) as well as the southern parts of the Scandinavian peninsula (present-day Norway, Sweden, and eventually Iceland). Most of our practices in heathenry come from the mythology and literature of these peoples—especially the *Prose* and *Poetic Edda*, which were written in Christianized Iceland.

For this reason and others, contemporary heathens have focused on Norse beliefs, rather than purely Germanic beliefs. The Nordic peoples were a cluster of tribes that lived in modern-day Denmark, Norway, and Sweden and were linked to the Germanic tribes but were culturally distinct in some ways. This focus on Nordic as both related to and distinct from Germanic peoples works for me, because heathenry is an expression of ancestor work for me, and many of my ancestors are Norwegian. However, if you would like to look at other kinds of Germanic beliefs and folklore, that is also well within the scope of heathenry. Nordic peoples shared the Scandinavian peninsula with the Sámi and Kven, and were often in conflict with those tribes, but they definitely influenced one another.

Here's where all of this cultural specificity becomes inclusive: you can learn it. There is no requirement within heathenry that you prove your ancestors hailed from Germanic people. If someone tries to tell you that, they are likely a literal neo-Nazi.[3] Mythology, literature, folklore, folk customs, language—all of these things can be learned. Culture is transmissible! Perhaps you are an immigrant living in modern-day Sweden and would like to connect with pre-Christian beliefs. Do it! Maybe you are a Black person who has always felt a strong connection with the Norse pantheon. You're welcome in my mead hall! If you are a queer person, there is so much within the lore for you specifically. Let's explore it together!

It is with this inclusive spirit that I use the terms "Norse" and "Nordic." I am describing beliefs, myths, legends, and folklore, all of which are available to you no matter who you are.

---

3   "Neo-Völkisch," Southern Poverty Law Center.

How to Use This Book

This book is a compilation of my own personal gnosis as well as my deeper academic research on runes and Nordic culture. This book is an invitation into the root culture of the runes, both in terms of myth and in terms of lived folkloric experience. There is a lot here, and it is likely that you will want to return to this book over time as you develop your own relationship with the runes.

I've already talked about the recent cultural history of runes, so we can move into the next few chapters ready to approach the path. This first chapter will talk about what it means to queer the runes. There was a time—not as long ago as many people assume—when the gender binary wasn't as strict. This is definitely true of Nordic people, and we can trace that through the literature of the Eddas, sagas, and grave goods. In this first chapter, I will be making the case for a queer understanding of the runes—based on both their history as well as their current uses for queer practitioners.

Then, I will talk briefly about queering Nordic magic and what that means in a grounded, ancestral practice. I think this is going to be one of the more controversial parts of this book, as well as one of the most important. We have a lot of conceptions about our ancestors, as people living in the 21st century, but their own ideas of queerness developed over the centuries. And not only that, as queer people—we break things. We break binaries, norms, stereotypes. A spiritual tool can work for us only if we find our way into that spiritual tool, if we can find a way of working it in our own contexts. So I'll be getting you acquainted with themes of Nordic magic, what that even means, and then talking about gender and sexuality as a part of Nordic magic.

After that, we'll get into individual rune study. This is going to be a wild ride! This is where the research that I've done will help you come to a place of understanding the traditional meanings, and then will help you to queer the runes in your own way. There will be a lengthy piece written by me about the meanings of each rune, as well as some lore associated with each rune, and then from there I'll talk about applying the lessons of each rune to our modern life.

The Three Ætts

I've structured the rune study by dividing them into three "ætts." While the ætt is a modern concept—dividing the Elder Futhark into three equal sections of eight runes—I've still decided to organize the rune chapters into the ætts. There are a couple of reasons for this: First, threes are important to heathenry. Three is the holiest number on this path. It's the number of the Norns, it's the number of Vanir living among the Aesir, it's the number of Loki's children. Threes show up constantly in Nordic culture—repetitions of three, "I saw three maidens" charms, even multiples of threes (six, nine) show up constantly as lucky numbers. Second, I find this structure useful for telling stories within the Futhark. It's how I learned the runes way back when, and I see a definite story in each of the ætts. The final reason is purely organizational: twenty-four micro chapters felt ridiculous, and one long rune chapter felt unmanageable.

This part of the book also contains journal prompts. These are meant to help you channel the energy of specific runes, to get to know their energy, as well as to use the runes to help you move forward in a

FIRST ÆTT

| Fehu | Uruz | Thurisaz | Ansuz |
| Raidho | Kaunaz | Gebo | Wunjo |

SECOND ÆTT

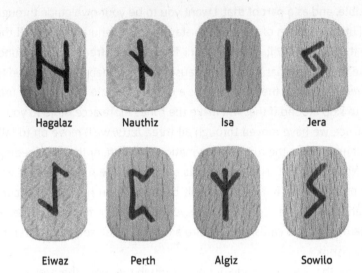

Hagalaz   Nauthiz   Isa   Jera

Eiwaz   Perth   Algiz   Sowilo

THIRD ÆTT

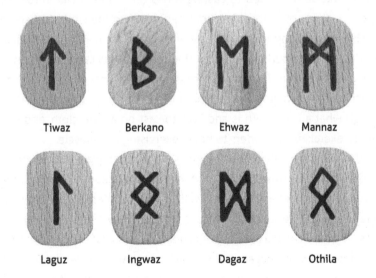

Tiwaz   Berkano   Ehwaz   Mannaz

Laguz   Ingwaz   Dagaz   Othila

journey of self-discovery. Your mileage may vary—between runes, or with the runes in general. I want to make these runes as accessible as possible, and as a part of that, I want you to be your own guide through the Futhark section of the book. If starting with Fehu and going all the way through to Othila doesn't work for you, feel free to skip around. While the Futhark has an order because it is an alphabet, it is not tied to a numeric order in the same way as a different oracle like tarot. So feel free to skip around if that will make the runes more accessible to you.

Once we have moved through all three ætts, we'll move on to talk about how to use the runes for divination. Spåcraft, or the art of seeing, in a Nordic context uses many tools outside of the runes, which I will also briefly cover. But first, you will begin to learn how to have conversations with the runes. They are very different in format from reading tarot or oracle cards, and require a different skill set and a different relationship.

Now that we have made our way through the runes themselves, it's time to start putting them together in readings that are more complex than single-rune pulls. Chapter 7 will cover a lot of the things that a new rune reader will need for practicing divination. A large portion of that chapter will be dedicated to casting runes on a cloth. I will introduce the cloth, different shapes the runes can make on the cloth, and some exercises for sinking into a more liminal space for reading. I will also include a sample reading or two so that the students can see this style of reading in action. This is an incredibly subtle form of rune reading and isn't often explained in depth. In this chapter, I will walk readers through what a rune cloth is and how to cast on a rune cloth, and will prepare exercises for readers to begin exercising this muscle.

After we have fully embodied each of the runes, we will move on to talk briefly about using the runes in magic. I'll talk about historic ways the runes were used in magic, as well as some contemporary takes on using them for spellcasting. Magic is actually how I first came to the runes—I would carve a rune into a candle to bless that candle with that rune's intentions. It's because of my magical relationship with the runes that working with them in divination came naturally. So in this section,

I will write about runic magic with a few rune spells to get you started and some exercises to help you write some of your own rituals.

This is a very exciting path to embark on! Make sure that you take time to yourself while reading this book, stay hydrated, move your body as much as you can, and listen to your dreams. The runes are a unique divination practice because they reverberate beyond the divination session. You'll begin finding them in nature, in the wild, in collages, sometimes even in clothing. Take note of the synchronicities as they come up! You may have a very different relationship to each of the runes than I do! This practice is deeply relational, and that's why there are journal prompts and activities provided for you for each rune along the way.

But my approach is only one way to do it.

This book isn't about the one true meaning of the runes—I don't think such a thing is possible. If you want a truly historical book, this also isn't it. This book is about discovery and building relationships with the runes. Your relationship will look different from mine, and that's okay and how it should be. I want to provide ample space for diversity of thought and growth within rune reading.

2

Queering the Runes

Queer (adj): not fitting traditional ideas about gender or sexuality, especially the idea that everyone is either male or female or that people should have sexual relationships only with the opposite sex

To be queer is to be liminal.

This book is dear to my heart because it fulfills a specific need I see in contemporary heathen and pagan literature: connecting our beliefs explicitly to a shared cultural understanding of queerness. Members of the LGBTQIA+ community are everywhere, in every faith and every culture—whether or not it is safe to be out. There is a huge subtext of queerness within the source texts for heathenry, and some scholars are beginning to look at these texts as potential sources of queer mythology instead of assuming heterosexuality and cisgender. The gods are promiscuous, the jokes are bawdy, there's a wink and a nod and a playfulness that remind me of the best of laughing at a drag show.

Queer is existing in defiance of heteronormative sexuality, and that places you outside of the norm. To be queer is to exist in a liminal space, both outside of and a part of society. I'm going to use the word "liminal" a lot throughout the rest of this book, so I want to take some time to talk about what I mean. Liminal is the space in between—it's transitional. The liminal can be physical (between places, between genders), emotional (like a period of grieving, or falling in love), or metaphorical (the fork in the road, the moment before you make a choice). Liminal: the world of the gods, the spirits, the otherworld entities is liminal by nature. The metaphoric liminal is a place that Odin himself very much exists within—he is the wanderer, after all, not the stationary king of the hall who stays in one place to oversee the operations of his kingdom. Instead Odin understands the most important thing he can do to protect his kingdom to be to wander. He finds wisdom in the margins. Odin is thirsty for knowledge, and sometimes the best source of that knowledge is very far outside of the grandest halls of the land. He is also known to bend the rules of gender presentation: He learns feminine magic, some of the idols that are left over from the Bronze Age show him in tradition- ally feminine garb, and he is mocked by Thor for sleeping with women and men in the Hárbarðsljóð.[1] Odin practices seiðr, which is considered "feminine magic," and is often referred to in explicitly queer terms in the mythology. It's known that Odin slept with men as well as women. And all of this is after the myths have gone through an early Christian filter—imagine how queer he was before! And even so, he still isn't the most overtly queer of the gods.

Loki is one of the most infamous gender traitors in the Eddas. Even those with a passing understanding of the Eddas has an understanding that Loki is far from a paragon of cisgendered heterosexuality. In fact, for the purposes of being as fluid as I can when discussing Loki, I will be using they/them pronouns to describe this being. Using gender-neutral pronouns allows me to talk about Loki in their multiplicity of gender expressions. Here are some examples just from the myths: Loki trans- forms into a mare and bears Sleipnir; they cross-dress (or transition?) consistently; they have both male and female partners.[2] Loki is more than a gender bender in the myths—they are the gender bender in Norse myth. The Eddas have always been a little queer, even if we hav- en't focused on it until recently.

The practice of magic itself is considered a liminal act. Magic exists somewhere between reality and the reality we are seeking to create; it is not real in that tangible sense but it is the creation of something

1   Jefford Franks, "Óðinn: A Queer Týr?
2   "Hárbarðsljóð," in Larrington, *The Poetic Edda.*

other-than-real in an attempt to impact reality. Contemporary occultists often create their own liminal space in which to perform magic—the ritual circle. In Norse culture being a magical practitioner shows that you are willing to take a step back and look at the Web of Wyrd, to really engage with the forces that are bending and twisting fate. This web is outside of human knowledge normally, and it isn't even managed by the gods—it is managed by a power higher than the gods. When Odin needs someone to provide him a reading to understand the future and what is coming in Ragnarök he consults a long-dead human völva[3]—which just shows the high esteem in which the wyrdworkers were held. To work with wyrd is to work outside of conventional expectations. It necessitates a certain level of fluidity that we can see in the myths about the gods and the stories we tell as a Nordic culture.

The conversation about gender and sexuality within Norse tradition is happening at the academic level, and it's happening within Norse pagan community (especially among those who worship Loki), but there is not a book that focuses purely on queering the runes themselves.

> *Queer (v): to change something so that it does not relate only to one gender, either male or female, or so that it no longer fits traditional ideas about gender or sexuality*

"Queer" is not just who you are, but it is *how* you are in the world. To queer something is to make space for queer people, to make heteronormativity that much less normal. To queer things breaks the binary: it breaks the firm definitions between genders, and it breaks apart the heterosexual expectations rooted in our culture. For queer people, to live our lives is to queer culture. In the academic world, queer theory takes its name from a derogatory term for persons considered "odd" or "abnormal," notably those whose sexual behavior, gender expression, or other characteristics do not conform to established social norms. It harnesses the experience and perspective of gender nonconformists and sexual deviants as a vantage point for understanding—and

---

3   "Völuspá," in Larrington, *The Poetic Edda.*

dismantling—the coercive workings of social structures and discursive regimes.[4] Queer readings of literature show us subconscious desires that may not have been considered appropriate at the time the piece of literature was written, but queering literature is also excavating the queer subconscious that runs parallel to mainstream culture. Queer people continue to live on in the great web of humanity, whether or not we are accepted.

This book is not only an act of revealing queer roots within heathen tradition, but it is also an act of queering modern heathen practice. As I mentioned earlier, there isn't really a single unbroken line of heathenry. There may be small family practices, but there hasn't been a long unbroken heathen faith. Whether heathens were converted by the sword or by treaty, the conversion made it dangerous to carry on their indigenous beliefs. The modern heathen revival is a creation of those who want to worship the old gods in an approximation of how our ancestors worshipped, but it will never be exactly the same way that our ancestors worshipped.

Queering heathenry means that we look deeply at our current practices and we find ways of melding queer culture and pagan culture. It's not terribly difficult to do—pagans also exist in a space outside of what many consider "normal society." Pagans and queer people meet in the margins. Queer heathens all over are already making practices that work for them, and my hope is that this book just provides more ideas and opportunities for spiritual growth where this is already happening. I don't want this book to be the last book on queering the runes, or on queering heathen practice. This book can and should be one part of a larger discussion that we have in our communities. But I do want this book to serve as a starting point.

Why do we queer heathenry specifically? Of course, anything can be queered and everything will be queered because queer people are everywhere. But it makes sense to queer heathenry for specific reasons that are rooted in the spiritual lessons of the tradition. I've already begun

---

4   Matzner, "Queer Theory and Ancient Literature."

to discuss how some of the gods are explicitly queer in the source texts, but there are other reasons that "queering" makes sense in this specific practice.

When I think about queerness, I think it is fundamentally about how we relate to one another. Whether we're talking about how people love (with passion that breaks expectations) or we're talking about gender (opening up to a myriad of expressions), everything comes back to how people relate with one another. You can be queer all on your own, but isn't it more delicious when we are queer together? Gay bars are places to gather, like the old mead halls of legend. Drag is a riotous show of gender transgression—but the point is that it's a show. It doesn't happen without an audience, and a safe audience isn't possible without community.

Heathenry is a very communal pagan religion.[5] If you're a solitary heathen that's totally okay, but so much of the basis for heathenry comes from how we relate to each other. Whether or not your community is a heathen community, a huge part of the values of heathenry lies in how we treat one another and form groups for mutual aid and community support. The *Hávamál* is one of our most important spiritual texts and much of the poem is about how we can relate to other people.[6] The sayings of the High One determine the best way to give gifts, receive visitors, give to others in society, how to simply be among other people.[7] For me, this means that heathenry is incomplete if we don't consider the ways that we interact with each other as well as the chosen community that so many queer people cultivate.

Engaging with queerness is baked into heathenry in ways distinct from other paganisms. I already mentioned the gender-bending that is present in the myths themselves. The thing is, this gender-bending is the tip of the iceberg. It's a queer fragment of what we know must have come before. The myths were written down after the conversion to Christianity, and therefore after certain changes in gender roles and

---

5 Lafayllve, *A Practical Heathen's Guide.*
6 Larrington, *The Poetic Edda.*
7 Larrington, *The Poetic Edda.*

binaries. The fact that so much gender-bending remains in the myths is truly incredible.

I don't want to extrapolate on artifacts we have lost; I don't want to read between lines that aren't there. However, as living heathens we have the opportunity to create new spiritual practices based on our contemporary culture. There are apartment-dwelling heathens who don't grow their own food but want to live in the rhythm of the land. There are vegetarian heathens. There are heathens who create rune art using new technology—drawing runes in programs on their computers rather than carving them in wood. And no religion should be totally static, in my opinion. We are constantly changing and evolving and learning more about how the world works—if religion is too stiff and unwilling to bend to the evolution of humanity, then that religion isn't able to be a true guide to the masses. So yes, we queer heathenry. We queer the runes. We queer witchcraft. Without queering, it is incomplete.

There's a reason I'm starting with "Queering the Runes." The runes themselves are ripe for this kind of work specifically because of what they are and how they operate on the magical plane. Runes are symbols that we have assigned meaning to in order to divine and learn things about the world. In my experience the runes are what you make of them, and for this queer witch, the runes are a welcoming space to explore identity, definitions, and pushing boundaries. They operate in a way that allows for expansiveness and shifts because they are more aligned with nature. Unlike my other primary divination practice (tarot), the runes don't depict people in any way. That allows us to see beyond the limits of our physical bodies and instead interpret the energy that is outside of the physical form. In not directly depicting any human or animal bodies, the runes are less likely to trip you up if you don't see yourself represented in them.

One thing that queer theory and runes have in common is the reliance on symbolism and abstraction. I promise I'm not going to get too far into technical queer theory in this part of the book, but I do want to take a moment to connect the academic tradition of queer theory outside of the academy. My academic training in literary criticism helped me to be able to interpret abstract symbols, which is why runes make sense to me as a diviner. I've also found that some of the headspaces and abstractions that I discovered in academia have been helpful for me to reframe how I view magical practice. This is a huge part of my work more generally speaking: I want to take these really incredible ideas out of the ivory tower. Whether those ideas are in the field of Viking and Medieval studies, queer theory, or linguistics, I want regular people to have access to them.

While queer people have always been here, queer theory as a way of understanding the world and analyzing culture is relatively new. It is not exactly an offshoot of feminist theory, but they are deeply related. Queer theory really emerged in the early 1990s and includes queer theorizations of text as well as theories about the nature of queerness itself.[8] Queering something means a process of disrupting, disturbing, and questioning the normal—that which is taken for granted. Queer theory, of course, centers itself around sexual and gender nonconformity, living outside of the cis-hetero-normative space. As Phil Hine writes in *Queerying Occultures*, "Queer sidles up to identities, ideologies; any category that's been taken to be timeless, solid and foundational, and exposes gaps, fissures, resistances, instabilities, different possibilities, and surprises."[9] By its very nature, queer theory works to complicate the things that we take for granted and make more space for the strange.

Semiotics is another field within critical theory that interacts with queer theory, but it is less well known. Semiotics is the study of signs and symbols as elements of communicative behavior.[10] It is the analysis of systems of communication as language, gestures, or clothing. And of course this is related back to queerness as so much of queer theory is about carving out the language with which to explain ourselves, and tracing that coded language through history. Things like clothing, slang, and even flower symbolism have been really important to the process of excavating queer symbols. This is also a huge part of the occult! You can probably already think about how this study of symbols is fertile ground for divination.

---

8 "Queer Theory," *Encyclopedia.pub.*
9 Hine, *Queerying Occultures.*
10 Baudrillard, *Simulacra and Simulations.*

Runes are also a process of semiotics: the modern rune worker tries to find meaning in symbols that were important to our ancestors, but that are not necessarily a part of our everyday lives anymore. These symbols can be taken at face value, but so much more often we need to massage them a bit to make sense. The runes are not a pictorial oracle, and while some of the shapes help us to understand their meaning, engaging in art analysis is not the way to get to the root of this oracle. We must see them as symbols, as representatives of a symbol, and as the vehicle for delivering the message. And the meanings of the runes themselves are influenced by the layers of culture and history connecting them in their historic moment to their contemporary use. The runes then take on a triple meaning: the meaning we know they had—a.k.a. the linguistic meaning, the meaning of our *imagined history* of the runes, and the contemporary meaning each rune worker creates as they work with them. All of these meanings are real and true.

The linguistic meaning of the runes is obvious. They are letters; the letters relate to sounds. You can write with the runes in a totally mundane way. There are countless archaeological findings of runes that were used as writing, and the contents of these rune findings aren't necessarily magical or even special in nature. During the Viking Age the runic inscriptions are more commemorative, with strictly regulated language that makes them easy to interpret.[11] However, the oldest inscription of proto-Scandinavian is *alu*, which could translate to *own* n. "beer" but could also be translated as "give strength" or "keep alive."[12] The mundane and the magical get connected to one another throughout the history of this language.

The imagined history of the runes is where we begin to weave our personal magic into this system. Part of the reason we tell stories and make cultural artifacts is in a desire to understand ourselves better and make meaning of the world around us. In order to make that meaning, we have to construct imagined histories. We all do this all the time— it's a part of what makes us human! We seek patterns, and we try to

11 Larsson, "Runes."
12 Larsson, "Runes."

understand those patterns, and in doing so we create narratives of why the world is the way it is.

Depending on where you are in the world, there is an imagined history of the Nordic people and the runes. There is the history that Nordic people learn in school: not just about the Vikings but about Denmark and Sweden at war, about Norway becoming independent from Sweden, about the various countries of Scandinavia reacting to important world events like World War II (WWII). The real history is not as exciting as the stories we've created in the collective about the frozen countries of the North.

I've noticed that the imagined history of Scandinavia often revolves specifically around the Viking Age, but that comprises really only three hundred years or so of cultural history—a brief moment in the grand scale of existence. Many of the stories that we have of the Norse gods date back before the Bronze Age, and after the Viking era there came a fascinating time of connecting with the broader world and integrating new ideas. But people in the United States[13] really seem to care about only that one era of Nordic history. The runes have been co-opted into a part of a system of symbols that add up to a mythic ideal that is removed from the actual reality of the Viking. The runes are an important part of the aesthetic and therefore represent this imagined world of the Viking. I could (and perhaps will) write an entire book about the impact of aesthetics on the occult, but for now I will limit myself to the definition of an aesthetic as a part of the symbol.

The word "aesthetic" has skyrocketed in popularity recently as people use it to describe the style aspects of specific subcultures. To have an "aesthetic" is to fit in with a specific online community. That's not the kind of aesthetics I'm talking about here. Aesthetics is the study and philosophy of art, and it is through aesthetics that we are able to explore the intersection of philosophy with art history, psychology, neuroscience, evolutionary biology, gender studies, and critical race theory.[14] Aesthetics puts language to the way that ideas are translated

---

13 I'm limiting my generalization to the United States because this is the only place I've lived.
14 Cahn, Ross, and Shapshay. *Aesthetics.*

through symbols, and therefore it has a great deal of influence on our understanding of culture. What we see with the Vikings in contemporary pop culture is a strong aesthetic communicated through historically inaccurate (but beautiful) costumes, lots of fur, Viking knotwork mixed with Celtic knotwork, dark/ambient/folk metal, tattoos, and a sculpted, muscular body type.

Of course these symbols are powerful, but they are not reality. I want to challenge us to look beyond the Viking as a symbol of Nordic history and culture. Yes, the Viking age was a time of great expansion and historic connection between Scandinavian people and the rest of the world. Yes, the Vikings did pillage and fight and die for honor. "Viking" was a lifestyle and the Viking Age is a span of a few hundred years—there is so much more to Nordic history than that. But the Viking is so powerful an archetype in the collective imagination that it comes to mind immediately when we think of runes. In my limited experience, many heathens were first drawn into this practice because of the aesthetic, and then discovered something that was really interesting and they wanted to engage with on a much broader scale. I urge you to get curious about other aspects of Nordic history and culture! Read the fairy tales! Watch contemporary Nordic film! Make yourself a smorgasbord! Constantly imagining the Norse people as conquerors and warriors with face paint and dreadlocks and fur-lined cloaks is creating a construct that is harsh. This is more than aesthetics: this is actively feeding the white supremacist egregore that Jung described in his infamous "Wotan" essay.[15] This is what I mean when I say that the runes are a part of an imagined history. And because it's an imagined history, we can choose something else.

The reality of the runes is the linguistic use, but the imagined history is what provides us with the magical basis for using them. And I don't mean that this is entirely made up; I don't mean to gaslight anyone in reading this. What I mean is that a lot of the magic that we have records of in the sagas and Eddas and literature can't necessarily be proven. The Nordic people had a habit of veiling meanings and using wordplay to allude to other myths and stories. In many cases, those

---

15 Jung, "Wotan."

myths and stories that were well known to the contemporary audience have been lost to time. So we fill in the blanks! We make sense of it through our own hoops and dreams of what this culture means. The imagined history is how we leap from the runes being used by Odin in the *Poetic Edda* to using them ourselves for our own needs. We are able to use the runes magically because we have written this imagined history on them.

But this imagined history isn't all wrong: imagination is incredibly important for magical operation. The important part of imagination is ensuring that you are creating healing archetypes. Each rune is related back to a theory or natural ally, and in my work with them they have taken on the role of spirit guides. What does "Horse" mean to you? What is a horse? What is a cultural construction of a horse? If a horse could give you wisdom, what would it say? These are the questions I ask when I'm building a relationship with the runes as archetypes—and these are the kinds of questions I'll be asking you as journal prompts throughout the book.

That is of course not to say that the runes aren't powerful—they are. In the sagas and Eddas, there are many warnings against working with runes for the novice. So rather than using this language of symbol and semiotics to downplay the importance that runes carry, I am using it instead to add power. The fact that they have that triple meaning (at least!) only adds to my deep respect and love for this oracle system. Once you have begun a relationship with the runes, your story about what they mean and where they come from is powerful. You'll begin seeing them everywhere, and when they jump out at you from tree branches, graffiti, leaves fallen on sidewalks, they will be an immediately recognizable support for you.

The runes are a very fertile ground for this kind of theoretical work, but there are also many ways that the very real history of Norse pagan culture and the mythology is explicitly queer. Figures like Loki and Odin, and magical practices like seiðr show that gender and sexuality were very different in the Viking age and earlier, which means there is not only an imagined history to draw from, but a very real history of queerness. Of course, the way we see the term "queer" today is wildly different from the ways people in the Viking age would have conceived of sexuality and gender. But we do have some clues as to how Nordic people throughout history defined gender and sexuality and how it worked. We even have historic manuscripts that cover what appears to be gender transition and fluidity outside of the fantastical mythology.

Hervarar saga ok Heiðreks is an actual medieval saga that depicts the life of someone who could very well be a trans man.[16] The saga is fascinating, and as with most sagas it covers the life of many people within a family. The section I'm most interested in centers around Hervǫr who was assigned female at birth but very much transitions socially into the role of a man.[17] Hervör is a tomboy from the start, and as he comes of age he goes to visit his kinsman's burial mound in Samsø. Here Hervör, raises the ghost of his dead father, and they speak for a long time until eventually his father yields the magical sword Tyrfingr to him. After this Hervör changes his name to Hervard and spends years on the open seas. Eventually Hervard (de?)transitions back to Hervör and marries Hǫfundr, son of Guðmundr of Glaesisvellir. They have two sons and the saga then moves on to follow those sons. Scholars are currently debating whether Hervör/Hervard maintained separate identities as a woman and a man throughout his life, or if this wasn't considered an example of transition as we think of it now.[18]

Academics studying Old Norse culture have approached the question of gender in many different ways in the past years. In her seminal work on the subject, Carol Clover writes about gendered descriptors in Old Norse and what they have to say about broader concepts of gender and sexuality. "Blauðr (soft and weak) and hvatr (bold or active) can be used for people regardless of their culturally constructed sex—what matters is their social power and status. Power is then the determinate for gender."[19] Hvatr is then considered what we traditionally think of as

16 For the sake of simplicity I will use he/him pronouns to describe Hervör/Hervard.
17 "Summary," *Hervara saga ok Heiðreks*. The Skaldic Project.
18 Hannah Burrows, "Anonymous Fornaldarsögur, Hervarar Saga Ok Heiðreks."
19 Clover, "Regardless of Sex."

"masculine," like going to war—and that can be applied no matter the physical construction of the body. Valkyries and Shield-Maidens have long fascinated us "modern" people—for they are fierce but feminine. They are in opposition to the modern concept of war as a masculine endeavor. But if we divorce the concept of masculinity from bodily sex, then it is not at all in opposition to the Valkyries' gender, because their gender is separate from their body, which is separate from their sexuality.

Clearly things were more fluid than we originally thought.

There are a couple of terms from Old Norse that are important for us to understand when looking at gender, sexuality, and magic in the Old Norse world. Before we go more deeply into the book, I want to talk about some Old Norse terms that could have denoted queerness and other-gendered-ness. The first term that's necessary for us to understand in the context of medieval Norse is *seiðr*. This is a form of sorcery that was tied to the ability to see the web of wyrd and make changes to the fates. This is the form of magic that the völva in *Völuspá* practices, the kind of magic that is said to be used to understand the great mysteries. As I've already talked about, wisdom was often denoted as feminine in the Old Norse texts. If my theory is correct, it would mean that the moments we have in the myths—specifically moments of Thor calling Odin "ergi" in *Hárbarðsljóð*—are insertions of prejudice on the part of medieval writers. We know that there was a lot lost from the years of rich oral literary tradition, and we also know that plenty of this was lost. Seiðr is one of the most important ways that we will engage with Nordic magic from a gendered and queer perspective. Much more on seiðr later.

The second term we need to define is *ergi*.

Ergi has been translated anywhere between a general "unmanly" to taking the "passive" role in male gay sex (a.k.a. bottoming). It was okay for a man to participate in sex with another man as long as he was the one doing the penetrating. Ergi is one of the most important words that we know from Old Norse specifically because it can be used to find behavior that would have been labeled as "queer" by contemporaries. Until the word "ergi" appears in the record, it is difficult to understand to what extent the Old Norse viewed homosexuality as "other."[20] However it's important that we not completely conflate "ergi" with our under-standing of gay men today, because the term comes from a very different culture. Within the cultural context of the Viking age, ergi was considered an insult, but it may have had deeper roots in connection with femininity more generally.

With the emergence of the term ergi, we have an understanding of queer sexuality as considered unusual and outside of the norm. It is here that queerness becomes strange, something unusual, something that an honorable man was not supposed to do. It's hard to know what is lost in translation when looking back at old texts like the *Prose Edda* and the *Poetic Edda*, but the presence of the word ergi allows us to track queer acts in the stories—and there are many. Odin himself is called ergi for his appetite for sexual partners of any gender—as well as his willingness to bend gender norms to satisfy that appetite.

Ergi also tells us the consequences for queer behavior from men in the Viking era. According to the Grey Goose laws (an Icelandic legal manuscript from around 1280), to call someone ergi was considered high defamation, and the person accused of ergi behavior was legally allowed to challenge them to a duel to the death. In murdering their accuser, the one accused of being ergi would prove their masculini-ty.[21] So this was a grave insult, but not quite in the way that "unman-liness" might be considered an insult today. I think it's interesting that "unmanliness" would be an insult, and I wonder if this focus on manliness and keeping gender roles connected to physical sex is a later development. There must be something lost in this translation, because the two things don't make sense when taken together. Then again, there are a lot of things that don't make sense about society today, or that would appear to be in direct contradiction. That's the thing about culture: it's messy.

---

20 Jefford Franks, "A Queer Tyr?"
21 Cahn, and Shapshay, *Aesthetics.* Sørenson, *The Unmanly Man.*

To all of this I say: we're taking back ergi. We're ergi and proud. We might be unmanly, but in the way that means we aren't participating in toxic masculinity.

To queer ergi is to find within this slur a common identifier with ancestors—much like how the LGBTQ community has worked to reclaim the word "queer."

3

A Radical Heathen's History of Runes

Now that we are properly contextualized, it's time to move on to the main reason we're all here: the runes themselves.

The Elder Futhark first emerged as an alphabet around the 2nd century. This is the first time we see this particular alphabet on artifacts that have survived—it is possible that they were in use earlier but that we haven't discovered artifacts with these runes preserved on them. Writing things down in this time was relatively rare—it took effort. The Germanic tribes were a largely oral society, so for the average person there wasn't much need to write or record things.

The linguistic and phonetic study of the runes is not something I'm going to do much of in this book, but there will be a diagram in each rune chapter about the sound the rune makes and its importance in the Futhark. This way you will be able to write in the runes if you want to, and that may even be an important part of the way you learn them and work with them. One really interesting exercise is to write your name in runes, and then look up the meaning of the letters. For example, my name is Siri, spelled ᛋᛁᚱᛁ. This translates to "Sun/Success, Ice, Wheel, Ice." It's a really interesting way of thinking of the energy that I carry with me.

Each rune is assigned a specific sound, and when you learn the sounds you can (mostly) write out English or any other language in the

Rune	Transliteration	International Phonetic Alphabet	Proto-Germanic Name	Meaning
ᚹ	f	/f/	Fehu	cattle, wealth
ᚢ	u	/u(:)/	Uruz	aurochs (or sleet)
ᚦ	þ | th	/θ/, /ð/	Thurisaz	giant
ᚨ	a	/a(:)/	Ansuz	"god," "breath," speech
ᚱ	r	/r/	Raidho	ride, journey
ᚲ	k(c)	/k/	Kaunan, kaunaz	ulcer, torch
ᚷ	g	/g/	Gebo, gyfu	gift
ᚹ	w	/w/	Wunjo	joy
ᚺ ᚻ	h	/h/	Hagalaz	hail
ᚾ	n	/n/	Nauthiz	need
ᛁ	i	/i(:)/	Isa	ice
ᛃ	j	/j/	Jera	year, good year, harvest
ᛇ	ï (æ)	/æ:/	Eiwaz	yew tree
ᛈ	p	/p/	Perth	well, luck, birth, pear tree
ᛉ	z	/z/	Algiz	elk, protection, defense
ᛊᛋ	s	/s/	Sowilo	sun, victory
ᛏ	t	/t/	Tiwaz	justice, the god Tyr
ᛒ	b	/b/	Berkano	birch tree
ᛖ	e	/e(:)/	Ehwaz	horse
ᛗ	m	/m/	Mannaz	man/humankind
ᛚ	l	/l/	Laguz	water, lake
◇ᛝ	ŋ, ng	/ŋ/	Ingwaz	the god Yng or Freyr, portal
ᛞ	d	/d/	Dagaz	daybreak
ᛟ	o	/o(:)/	Othila	heritage, estate, legacy, family

alphabet. The sounds are a little different—Old Norse has some sounds that we don't use, and vice versa—but they are still usable. The table on page 30 shows the runes, their transliterative and phonetic correspondences, as well as the meaning of the rune.

The Elder Futhark is the runic alphabet we use most often today (and the one that I will be writing about in this book). However, as languages grow and change so do the means of recording them. The oldest rune stone with the full Elder Futhark in order is from the Kylver Stone found on a farm in Gottland and is dated back to roughly 400 AD.[1] Starting in the 5th century, the Anglo-Saxons and Frisians expanded the Futhark to include an additional five runes. Beginning in the late 8th century in Scandinavia the Elder Futhark was reduced to the Younger Futhark. This happened at the same time as developments in language actually expanded the vowel sounds and phonemes used. It later did expand again to include a symbol for each phoneme. I am not equipped to really get into an explanation of this particular contraction and expansion— but I do find it interesting. Medieval manuscripts began to combine uses of the Elder and Younger Futharks, until the Younger Futhark prevailed.

There are many different kinds of artifacts that include the runes. There are large rune stones that sit in open fields, runes carved into different artifacts, as well as much shorter "rune sticks" such as the rune sticks that were discovered in Bryggen.[2] Most of the rune sticks that we still have are lists, perhaps short letters. There are some that come from the Bergen collection that we know were spells. The Bergen rune charm, which was discovered in 1955, was among nearly 670 runic inscriptions discovered.[3] This find was incredible because it gives us an incredible glimpse into medieval witchcraft. The rune stick itself is a long stick with four roughly equal sides, and text was carved on each side—a spell intended to ensnare a man. The Bergen rune charm is an example of magic in action. Most of these runic talismans haven't survived because they were made of wood, which

1 Spurkland, *Norwegian Runes.*
2 "Bryggens Museum," *Bymuseet.*.
3 Herteig, "The excavation of Bryggen, Bergen, Norway."

decomposes and burns and is otherwise fragile to the ages. Examples like the Bergen rune charm give us a window into these traditional forms of witchcraft.

The meaning of the Elder Futhark was lost in Scandinavia for centuries, because the medieval manuscripts were written in the Younger Futhark. The Elder Futhark was deciphered by the Norwegian scholar Sophus Bugge in 1865.[4] To place this in history, this was after the rise of Norwegian Romantic Nationalism, which led to Norway becoming independent from Sweden.[5] It's important to note because of the political implications for Norwegians at the time, which meant people were really looking for things to rally around to create a national identity. In the name of their independence, it was becoming ever more essential to reclaim culture that had been lost, which drove scholars in this field and led to an increase in interest in Old Norse linguistics.

This mix of nostalgia for the past, with the creation of a new national identity is extremely potent. It helps us to understand how the runes have been used by white supremacists, and therefore we can understand better how to divorce them from white supremacy.

Confronting White Supremacy in the Rune Magic Revival

We look to the past to gain perspective, and to learn from our mistakes. That's why I study history, why I search for a historic basis in my folk magic. I want to understand all the factors that led us to this moment in time. This is a theme that runs through my work as an activist as well as my work in witchcraft. The occult often runs parallel to history: developments in ideas behind closed doors, in the shadows, impact what happens in broad daylight. As witches, we know this; If we didn't, we would have a hell of a time casting spells.

This is especially true of the runes, in my experience. As an alphabet, they go through a lot of transformations and transmutations in their long history. They also trace the changes in Nordic culture in

4 Hill, "Futhark."
5 Salvesen, "The Historian as Architect of Nation."

interesting ways. One major consensus of all occult authors writing about runes and Norse paganism is a draw to reconstruct these runes, that they are mystical and magical in themselves and therefore it is necessary to work with them. The runes themselves are a compelling story, one that continuously draws in new practitioners. Much like Odin, heathens are constantly seeking new knowledge and under-standing of our shared past.

Knowledge is power. And knowledge is also a tool that can be used and shaped to fit a narrative that isn't the whole truth. This is espe-cially true when we can't know what these practices were exactly—the more authority someone can put into their work and their words, the more likely they are to be believed. If we allow the powerful to rewrite history—without examining that history—we are ill-equipped to truly learn. And at the same time, the people who have written heathen books, those who have been reconstructing heathen rituals since the 1800s, had their own agendas. So we have to study not only the pre-Christian heathen practices, but the more modern movements that have brought us to heathenry today.

Sometimes, this will mean reading sources written by people that you don't agree with in order to analyze the story they're telling. Yes, read the difficult histories, and always have your red pen handy. Question things. Read Black and Indigenous historians, and then look at the other history texts and you can see what they're covering up. Go deeper. It is essential to do this research to interrogate the reasons white suprema-cists seem comfortable to wrap heathen aesthetics around themselves.

For our history today, I'm going to start in the 1800s. As I mentioned earlier, this is a really pivotal time for European cultural identity. That philosophy and shift led to the appropriation of runes into a white supremacist's fantasy. After the fall of Napoleon, what we now know as Germany became a collection of thirty-nine sovereign states.[6] In 1848, the German people started to push for revolution and reform. After the conclusion of a couple of wars (with Denmark and Prussia), the Northern

---

6 Office of the Historian of the United States. "Issues Relevant to U.S. Foreign Diplomacy: Unifi-cation of German States." *history.state.gov/countries/germany*.

German States were unified in 1862 by Otto von Bismarck.[7] He was able to situate Germany as a nation in itself through negotiations with individual heads of state and brought peace to warring regions (Prussia versus Denmark as well as victory in the Austro-Prussian war). The 19th century was characterized within the area we know of as Germany as a time of political gains, but also economic instability, the industrial revolution, and war.

This is important because it sets the stage for the Weimar Republic and the Nazi takeover.

As the Germanic states were uniting, people were trying to create a unified culture. And this wasn't happening only in Germany, it was happening across Europe as a part of the European Romantic Movement of the 1800s. The movement led to an interest in what makes Germany unique among European nations, as well as a revival in interest in mythology. Wagner's *Ring* cycle (*Der Ring des Nibelungen*) debuted in 1871, at the height of these unification efforts. This is one example of how Norse mythology was at the center of the Germanic imagination. And of course, it's important to bear in mind that this is a constructed, imagined history in the service of creating a Germanic nation-state.

Notably, this is also the time when the concept of race as we know it was being solidified in academic circles. Anthropology looked very different from how it looks today. The study of anthropology in the 19th century was essentially a system of categorization of people under a hierarchy.[8] Many anthropologists used their discipline to argue that slavery of African people was justified. To do this, they circulated the idea of European/white superiority. The different nations of Europe were even filtered into different levels in the hierarchy: Irish and Italians at the bottom, English and Germans at the top.[9]

This fed into an emerging theory of Germanic and distinctly North-Western European identity as a sort of "master race," superior to others. The concept of the "Übermensch," or "overman," is the result of this. The Übermensch is basically a concept within philosophy that the

---

7   Atkin, *The Wiley-Blackwell Dictionary.*
8   Baker, *From Savage to Negro.*
9   Baker.

human race is evolving, and that some people have evolved faster than others but that the Übermensch is a goal that all people can attempt to meet.

Here's an oft-cited quote from *Thus Spoke Zarathustra*:

You have made your way from worm to man, and much in you is still worm. Once you were apes, and even now, too, man is more ape than any ape . . . The overman is the meaning of the earth. Let your will say: the overman shall be the meaning of the earth . . . Man is a rope, tied between beast and over-man—a rope over an abyss . . . what is great in man is that he is a bridge and not an end.[10]

White supremacists to this day use this philosophical concept as a sort of "intellectual proof" that they have evolved beyond other races. Hitler was convinced that the Aryan race is the end of this progression—that the Übermensch is exemplified in the German race. White supremacists believe that this is the ideal everyone should strive for, but it is also an ideal that is only truly available to people with Germanic ancestry.

So what we've got in the 19th century is a perfect storm of racism and the development of white supremacy, all centered around Germanic culture and ideals. Anthropologists upholding Anglo-Saxon and Germanic blood as "superior," philosophers spreading the idea that there is a master race, as well as the unification of Germany and search for a Germanic identity all led to an increased interest in Germanic-Nordic mythology by white supremacists. This culminated in the Völkisch movement, and the imagination of a superior, white, German nation state.

The Germanic legends themselves became the source for what the "ideal" person was. The Völkisch movement rewrote history, drawing on the mythic cycles, folklore such as the Brothers Grimm, and medieval epics to create a fantasy Europe superior to all other continents. At the same time, scholars were drawing on a racialized version of the medieval past. The Elder Futhark code was cracked, invigorating interest in

---

10 Nieztsche, *Thus Spoke Zarathustra*.

runes. This historic and cultural milieu leads us right up to the eve of World War I (WWI). In the German Revolution of 1918, Emperor Wilhem II abdicated his position and Germany was declared a Federal Republic.[11] New leadership signed the Treaty of Versailles, accepting defeat and losing 13 percent of its territory and all colonized territory in Africa and the South Sea.[12] Communists seized power in Bavaria, and a new currency was minted.

It was deeply humiliating for them to lose so dramatically.[13] The Germans had built themselves up as the epitome of human evolution, the ideal every other nation should strive for. But the myth of the German superpower, and the idea that the Germans would rise again, was essential for building up the willpower to start another global struggle. Odin had been venerated since the 19th century, and one of the rallying points for German racists was the mythic return of Odin. This is also when we see the runes and other pre-Christian Germanic symbolism used explicitly to confirm supposed "racial superiority." The Thule Society was founded shortly after WWI, which was an explicitly völkisch group that focused on Germanic occult works.[14] The Thule Society centered around a blood claim to the Aryan race. Members had to sign a declaration that neither themselves nor their wives had any Jewish or "colored" blood. The Thule Society was one of the primary sponsors of the Deutsche Arbeiterpartei, or German Worker's Party, which was eventually reorganized into the Nazi Party.

It was in the Weimar era that German youth also began to call their völkisch beliefs Odinist. They were encouraged by older Germans who participated in the völkisch movements. According to Jeffrey Kaplan, it wasn't just local Germans but "sympathizers abroad whose anti-Semitic beliefs would lead them to conclude that, as Christianity is built on a Jewish foundation, it too must be swept away in the construction of a millenarian 'New Order.'"[15] This New Order would be built upon a

---

11 Boemeke, Feldman, and Glaser, *Versailles*.
12 "German Territorial Losses, Treaty of Versailles, 1919." United States Holocaust Memorial Museum.
13 Boemeke, Feldman, and Glaser..
14 Burley, "Rainbow Heathenry."
15 Kaplan, "Right-Wing Violence in North America."

Germanic past that never existed—it was purely imagined by white supremacists.

Out of this growing spotlight on Odin in German youth gangs, Carl Jung wrote what is his most controversial work: "Wotan."[16]

Jung worked with the idea that deep beneath our consciousness rests a dream world filled with archetypes. These archetypes have something to teach us, and they inspire action in our daily lives. Jung was watching the Hitler Youth and the rise of fascism in Germany, and wrote "Wotan" to process that rise. He connects the archetype of Odin the wanderer, the magician that moves through the world and stirs up magic and creates unrest, with the spread of the Hitler Youth. Jung went on to write about how this surge in violence in Germany was because of the reawakening of Odin within the bloodlines of German youth. While this wasn't the first connection drawn between Odin and German nationalism, it was the most widely read—especially outside of Germany.

"Wotan" evocatively connected Odin with Hitler, something the Nazis had been trying to do for years at this point. Jung also wrote that militarism is unique to the Germanic spirit: Wotan, the warrior/wanderer, was the archetype that he used to bring this all together. This has long been another misunderstanding of pre-Christian Germanic and Norse culture. Yes, it was a warrior culture during the Viking era, but there were many more people home on the farm than those who went marauding, and the mass adoption of Viking trade came because of other difficult politics at home.[17] As World War II raged, Nazis continued to misuse Norse symbols. One of those myths of a Viking past was the Männerbünde—this idea that there was a cultural continuity between the Nazis and secret warrior bands composed of young men who had undergone religious-ecstatic initiation rites.[18] The theory was widely popularized by Otto Höfler, a German academic who studied German literature, culture, and history beginning in the 1920s.

His research directly inspired the structure of the SS and the SA, which both relied on Odinist symbolism in their initiation rituals and

---

16 Jung, "Wotan."
17 Hartsuyker, "We Shouldn't Let."
18 Burrell, "Otto Höfler's Männerbund Theory."

cosmology.[19] These are inventions of the Nazi party, not rituals that are true to pre-Christian heathenry.

Post-WWII to the Present

After World War II, Odinist ideas were resoundingly discredited in Germany—from a political perspective. However, in West Germany there was a freedom of gathering and religion, and so Odinism shifted from being a broader cultural force into a more religious force. Incorporating into Asatru meant that white supremacists who believed in the toxic völkisch ideas could gather to discuss their ideas and stay connected even as the German nation punished outright Nazism.[20] This is still how these white supremacist ideas are spread today: white supremacists gather in prison under the guise of Odinism, but are actually organizing their hatred and bigotry toward acting on it outside of prison. This trend spread throughout Europe, and into the Americas. Many white supremacist groups operating in America today organize under and around Norse imagery.

Else Christianson, a Danish immigrant to America after WWII, founded the Odinic Fellowship. This was explicitly based on the concept of Nordicism—an idea that the Nordic peoples were a subspecies of humanity superior to other races. Remember how Nietzsche's idea of the ubermensch and the race theory in anthropology developed simultaneously? Nordicism is a direct result of that. Else Christianson began teaching Odinism to others, and writing about it. She especially targeted prisons as a recruitment ground.[21]

This is where Stephen McNallen and the Asatru Free Assembly come into play. McNallen is a known white supremacist and far-right extremist who founded some of the first Asatru organizations in the United States. His ideologies and teachings revolve around this idea of Nordicism, the German soul, that this is not an open religion but one that you must be born into by blood.[22] The name for this? Metagenetics.

---

19 Kaplan, "The Reconstruction."
20 Burley, "Rainbow Heathenry."
21 Burley.
22 Burley and Smith. "Asatru's Racist Missionary."

Metagenetics is a concept that bolsters Stephen McNallen's politics and "spiritual" group. The concept defines culture as being passed down genetically between descendants.[23] In the theory of metagenetics, only those who are the literal, direct ancestors of a tradition may tap into the collective ancestral knowledge within that tradition. McNallen has attempted to justify this position in the past, pointing to Native American spiritual traditions that are closed. But he staunchly refuses to recognize the power differential: While Native people are attempting to protect their spirituality from brutal colonization and erasure, McNallen's brand of Asatru denies the humanity of anyone outside the mythic "Aryan race."

Now, the Asatru Free Assembly was not just the work of Stephen McNallen. Other leaders of the organization included Robert Stine, a former member of the KKK and a US Nazi Party Member, as well as Valgard Murray, a former Nazi Party member. These men have beat up openly gay men who came to AFA meetings, and have a strict policy that people are ready to put their bodies on the line and use violence to meet their goals. The Asatru Free Assembly was dissembled and then reborn as the Asatru Folk Assembly.

There are other white supremacist groups that proliferate today, operating under the aesthetic of Asatru.[24] The Vinlanders Social Club—a.k.a. Thug Reich—use violence to control people they perceive as the enemy. A lot of these groups—both in Scandinavia and in North America—see immigration as a primary threat to whiteness in their countries. The Soldiers of Odin state that it is their mission to "protect citizens from refugees through vigilante street patrols."[25] Many of the groups active in North America, such as the Vinlanders Social Club and the Wolves of Vinland, use the concept of Vinland as their rallying cry.

Vinland was a failed Viking settlement in North America in the 10th century. Two Icelandic sagas remain that discuss Vinland, but they disagree over the details. Basically, the Vikings fought with the indigenous people, lost, and left. This may seem like a strange rallying point—why

---

23 Burley and Smith.
24 Weber, "White Supremacy's Old Gods."
25 "Bridge Initiative Factsheet: Soldiers of Odin," Bridge Initiative..

celebrate a failure?—but as Weber writes in "White Supremacy's Old Gods,"[26] Vinland allows white supremacists to speak of the past as both victors and victims. Weber goes on to assert that Vinland also allows Odinists to assert a historical claim over North America: they are able to claim some level of indigeneity, while maintaining and emphasizing their Northern European roots. Anytime a group of heathens references Vinland, be on your guard for white supremacy—unless, of course, they are talking about the Vinland saga or warning others to steer clear of ideological Vinland.

I'm talking about these groups specifically so that you know what to look out for and how to avoid them. The more knowledge about the different sects of white supremacist gangs who use the runes, the easier it is to avoid them. As the uprising sparked across the country following George Floyd's murder, many white supremacist groups poured into Minneapolis and many other cities. Certain runes are brandished on the flags of these groups, like Tiwaz and Othila, as well as other Nordic symbols, like the Valknut. Please know that, when and if you see these on white supremacist flags, they are stolen symbols, twisted from the path of healing into a symbol of hatred.

I have no friendship with fascism.

So after all of that, why study the runes?

What does this all mean for contemporary antiracist heathens?

We will cede no ground to fascists. When Norse immigrants to the US assimilated, we gave up our cultural identities for whiteness, and learning more about our root culture is taking a stand against the homogenizing force of whiteness and chipping away at the armor of white supremacy. The perversion of white supremacists abusing Nordic folk culture must end. We need more women, more queer people, more people of color, more leftists working with the runes and heathen

---

26 Weber, "White Supremacy's Old Gods."

culture. In order to do that, there need to be safe places to learn, which is why I teach about runes and why I wrote this book.

When you get to the roots of these practices, there is a deep beauty to be found—whispers of ancestral knowledge, passed down in poetry and mythology for centuries. It is so completely different from the fantasy that white supremacists engage with that the two ideologies don't compare. This path has been deeply healing for me and for many others, and it is time to shine a light on the beauty that can spring from the Nordic path.

The thing that stands out to me as the greatest power of the runes and Norse mythology in general is the constant striving toward death and rebirth, a never-ending transformation. The Ragnarök cycle is astounding in its beauty. What I craved for so long growing up was an admission that the gods themselves are fallible creatures, and I see that reflected over and over again in the Norse cosmos. Even the Allfather fails to stop the gods' ultimate reckoning, try as he might. Ragnarök happens precisely because of the gods' hubris. The gods fall long before the actual battle: it's a fall from their own ethics. They aren't living up to their own standards, and therefore Ragnarök becomes inevitable. It's the necessary death, making way for a new age of gods.

We're living during Ragnarök times. It feels like this mythic cycle is pressing closer and closer, that these end times are coming. The ultimate hope of Ragnarök is that three figures will come back and create the world anew, spinning it from golden flax. It is this cycle of dramatic death and rebirth that helps me when times feel really dark. I don't necessarily believe in fate. I don't believe that we have no control over what happens, how our lives play out, any of that. I think that fate works through showing us options. But we ultimately make the decisions—and so does everyone else along the way.

The runes are a way of helping us make those right decisions. They help us connect to our deeper selves. A lot of tarot readers or other occultists will say that you turn to tarot to get to know your higher self. I turn to runes because I want to learn my bones. The runes connect my interest in history, in how we got to where we are now, and keys for a postcapitalist, climate-resilient society. The runes call us in, they gather us and tell us the old stories, but they also know simultaneously that the old world has to die. I look back to look forward with clarity.

4

The First Ætt

FEHU

Keywords: prosperity, abundance, cattle, fee

Fehu is often interpreted as wealth or property. It is the first rune of the
Elder Futhark, and looks like a capital F with the two lines pointing up
instead of out. The sound is the "f" sound, like at the beginning of the
word Futhark. In fact, "FUTHARK" is just a way of saying the sounds of
the first six runes in rapid succession. The word itself is an abbreviation
for the alphabet. (Much like "alphabet" is a combination of the first two
Greek letters: alpha and beta.)

I think it's interesting and worth exploring that the entire Futhark
begins with this idea of wealth, property, or cattle. In the occult, the
order of things matters. So why do we start here? The major arcana in
a tarot deck are in a very specific order, and they tell a beautiful story
from start to finish. Rune scholars have also attested that the runes tell
a story, that the three Ætts of the Futhark have their own story to tell. If

the Fool is the initiation to the major arcana in tarot, Fehu is the initiation to the rune song.

But to my ears, there's a dissonance at the beginning of this song.

If the heathen's journey begins with wealth, what does that say about the priorities of this spiritual practice? The subconscious implication is that, because Fehu is the beginning energy, there's a prerequisite for a certain level of wealth needed to unlock the door to deeper levels of wisdom. On the face of it, that might seem like gatekeeping. "You must have a certain level of wealth to learn the mysteries." A lot of the pagans I know come to paganism precisely because they were tired of feeling like they needed a certain level of wealth to be accepted in their spiritual communities.

Contrary to this idea of wealth first, in my work with Odin and Freyja both deities have been magnanimous, generous, and ultimately supportive—especially in times of scarcity. Their presence is supportive and constantly reminds me that there is more to life than the immediate and often scary financial reality that comes with living under late-stage capitalism.

Fehu as a gateway for the Futhark, then, has a meaning deeper than wealth.

I think often about Fehu in connection with Maslow's hierarchy of needs: if Fehu is the initiation rune, it also speaks in some way to the conditions necessary for further growth. For example, if you are struggling daily to cover your basic needs, it will be difficult to focus on a new spiritual path. It's difficult to focus on a new spiritual path if you need to focus on the basics like food, shelter, and clean water. Fehu represents the conditions necessary to move forward on your spiritual path. It isn't an overabundance of wealth, but rather an understanding that we all have basic necessities. If those aren't being met, it's difficult to do the hard work of inner exploration.

I already mentioned that my relationship with the Norse gods is supportive and generative. They support me in stepping back from intense shadow work and trials when I need to. Because I work with them regularly, and because I work with the runes regularly, it's like they know I'll be back. Instead of demanding penance and work, the gods know that sometimes we need to sort things out in the material world before we can delve into things in the spiritual realm.

The wealth of Fehu isn't a gatekeeping sort of wealth; it is the recognition that we must have our basic needs met.

Heathens are very practical people. As I'm working with my own teachers, the things that keep coming up are things like "How can you simplify it so it's easy to show up and do the work you need to do?" Instead of casting a full circle, meditate on the tree of life. Instead of complicated tarot spreads, throw some runes down on a cloth and see what happens. Listen to the gut instinct that is at your core, and learn from there. We have the tools that we need within us, but spending too much time going within means that we may be neglecting the real-world impacts of our work. It's a balance. Frigg, Odin's wife and goddess of wisdom, constantly reminds me to make the magical practical.

So much of studying the runes is trying to understand the mindset of an ancient culture. So much of Old Norse culture was lost, and most of our source texts are written post-Christianization and therefore have been edited to contain some Christian ideals. So we need to attempt to go back to a time when Fehu didn't simply mean money, a time when exchange didn't mean what it does now. Fehu's wealth is not the wealth of our capitalist society—it comes from before capitalism. In my experience this is more reciprocal in nature: it's more about barter, what you can exchange, and about people figuring out how to get their needs met. Reframing Fehu as a symbol of barter, of exchange, shows there's an assumption of generosity inherent in the spirit of the rune. Rather than being about hoarding wealth in a contemporary sense, it becomes about having something that fulfills both your own needs as well as someone else's.

We'll talk about this more as I go further into the Futhark, but what I am increasingly learning from my heathen teachers is that Old Norse culture was based on the necessity of reciprocity and generosity. There were laws—well past the middle ages—that encouraged people to take in those in poverty. Between October 14 and December 14 the farm needed to get a lot of work done, and people would usually strive to have all their help for the winter hired by October 14th to ensure that everyone's needs would be met for the coming winter.[1]

There is something deep in the culture of Scandinavia about taking people in from the cold. You can see it in how many stanzas of the *Hávamál* deal with the responsibility to take in wanderers, and the mutual respect necessary in hosting.[2] There was so much etiquette built into giving and receiving gifts that we know this culture focused on generosity, rather than on hoarding wealth.

There are other elements to this rune, especially as we get into the complexities of the gods. The Aesir are often thought of as gods of Society, whereas the Vanir are more akin to gods of Nature.[3] The Vanir are thought to be deeply creative, focusing on arts and agriculture. They are gods of abundance. In the *Völuspá*, the völva tells the story of how the war between the Aesir and the Vanir broke out. Gullveig, a witch who sought gold in the realm of the Aesir, was burned three times and reborn three times, sparking a war between the two families of gods. Later, as the gods called a truce, Njord, Frey, and Freyja were sent from the Vanir to live with the Aesir as hostages who ultimately made Asgard their home. Many scholars have suggested that Gullveig is in fact Freyja in disguise.[4]

Connecting Fehu to Gullveig opens the rune up for interpretation as both generative and destructive. In its generative form, Fehu is an expression of our creative fire, bringing us closer in alignment with our life's purpose and how that creative fire can create abundance in our communities. However, in the destructive aspect, Fehu reminds us that wealth can corrupt, that it can cut ties and leave us isolated from community.

In a positive form, wealth can certainly generate more wealth— when you have your bases covered, you are more able to invest time in beautiful things, like art, music, writing, seeking meaning behind life.

1   Miller, "The Primstav Explanations."
2   Larrington, *The Poetic Edda.*
3   Smith, *The Way of Fire and Ice.*
4   Kvilhaug, *The Seeds of Yggdrasil.*

Rune	Transliteration	International Phonetic Alphabet	Proto-Germanic Name	Meaning
ᚠ	f	/f/	Fehu	cattle, wealth

ANGLO-SAXON RUNE POEM:

> *Wealth is a comfort to all men;*
> *yet must every man bestow it freely,*
> *if he wish to gain honour in the sight of the Lord.*

ICELANDIC RUNE POEM:

> *Wealth*
> *source of discord among kinsmen*
> *and fire of the sea*
> *and path of the serpent.*

NORWEGIAN RUNE POEM:

> *Wealth is a source of discord among kinsmen;*
> *the wolf lives in the forest.*

Opportunities for Ancestral Discovery

Think about the amount of care that would have gone into a relationship with cattle. Animal husbandry is a different level of attention and love than we typically apply to our work these days. It was also a very intensive kind of work that shouldn't be put off easily. How can you apply this level of care to the tools you work with now? How can you build a relationship with the work you do that allows you to live your life?

Think about the way your ancestors may (or may not) have had the resources they needed to thrive. Some of us come from very comfortable families, while others were fighting for survival. What's more, this can change through the centuries, and a family that was once struggling can have a better outlook now, or they could have lost great wealth. What were the most important resources for your ancestors one hundred years ago? Five hundred? How has this reverberated into your life now?

QUEER FEHU

We don't really use cattle as currency anymore, so we need to think about this rune from the current-day perspective of money and wealth. That is, however, an extremely loaded question for a lot of reasons. Often queer people are shut out of traditional means of acquiring money, or we may have family money and support withheld by homophobic family members. There's also the idea of "abundance guilt," when we have an abundance of cash and are still aware of the unjust way capital is distributed and feel guilty over our own comfort. There are *a lot* of reasons, in other words, that we might have complicated relationships with finances. These journal prompts will help you get to the root of some of your money issues and tap into the healing power of Fehu.

- What relationship would you like to have with money? And how does that differ from the relationship you currently have with money?

- What labor do you do that you are paid for? What labor do you wish you were paid for? How can you make those two things match up?

Fehu + Gyfu + Mannaz gets us to mutual aid. Fehu represents having enough money to dive deeper into your spiritual world and consider generosity. Gyfu is reciprocity and generosity. Finally, Mannaz represents community and the connections we share. How can you apply the idea of Fehu—that you have enough to spare—to your own mutual-aid projects? The obvious answer is to dedicate funds to mutual-aid projects, but there are times when *you* need the mutual aid yourself. Where is the balance now?

URUZ

Keywords: ox, strength, healing, conviction

This can be a difficult rune to connect with, especially for femmes. Under patriarchy, the word "strength" has a masculine connotation. And that is certainly the case with the over-masculine, hyped-up version of the Vikings we see in pop culture today. Too often when people think of "heathen" and "strength" together, some image of a big hulky man with face paint, blonde dreads, and vaguely tribal tattoos shows up in the imagination. If we do think of women and strength in this context, they are often attempting to emulate that masculine aesthetic. But strength is gender-neutral: anyone of any gender or presentation can be strong. Uruz has challenged me in so many ways, but most importantly this rune has led to a revelation about gender.

I want to take a moment to talk about the strengths of masculinity when separate from toxic masculinity.

Years ago, when I was working with Jeff Hinshaw in the Brooklyn Fools Tarot Immersion, we were talking about the Emperor as an archetype of divine masculine. It is so hard to visualize the divine masculine because we don't really have current day examples of it. Most of the very masculine archetypes we have now are steeped in the heterosexist patriarchy. And if there *are* examples of "Good Dudes" in pop culture, they aren't often divine figures. Divinity has a different connotation from standard human masculinity. Personally, one of the most important signifiers to me that a man is attempting to avoid toxic masculinity is that he is comfortable with femininity and being perceived as soft.

I would like to offer the idea that Uruz represents the divine masculine as well as the divine feminine and divine agender: divine masculine because of its association with strength, divine feminine because of the association with Auðhumla, and divine agender because all of these things are possible regardless of gender.

Uruz is our gateway into wild energy, the primal strength we can gain in working with the runes. Tauring talks about how Fehu is the domestic cattle, but Uruz is the wild ox that the cattle are descended from.[5] Nestled in between a rune of domesticity (Fehu) and a rune of primal, wild nature (Thurisaz), Uruz acts as a bridge between energies. Fehu is therefore a sense of cultivated wealth, of things that you work hard for, of daily routine that leads to abundance. Fehu is the energy of wealth, of having enough to build off of. Uruz is the energy of a stubborn being, of transformation of the self through hard work. Uruz represents a very special kind of ox. The wild aurochs, now extinct in Europe, holds a special place in the Norse mythic landscape. Uruz sits at the crux of these opposites in more ways than one. There is a wildness to these creatures, but they are not completely separate from us.

The most famous aurochs in Norse mythology is Auðhumla. Some say that she was the first being to be released from the ice—created when the primal fires met the ice, Auðhumla stepped forward to nourish other beings. Auðhumla is also said to have fed and nourished the giant Ymir, the howling sound at the beginning of time.[6] She licked the first god, Búri, from the ice. Búri is the Grandfather of Odin, Vili, and Vé, who went on to kill Ymir when he refused nourishment to others. They divided up his body and from it carved the nine realms.

In this way, this ancient cow is an active creator and matronly figure. You could even argue that she is the beginning of nourishment in Norse myth and therefore the mother of all of us. Auðhumla springs from the stubborn elements of fire and ice, the clash of Muspelheim and Niflheim. Uruz finds a middle way, not too warm and not too cold, and brings life from the ice without burning it. Uruz finds a middle way in terms of our gender identities as well: we can all see ourselves in this rune, whether we are masculine, feminine, or those edgewalking nonbinary folks.

---

5 Tauring, The Runes.
6 Kvilhaug, The Seed of Yggdrasil.

But Uruz is more than nourishment—it is also a rune of the hunt. Joseph Campbell wrote:

> In the hunting cultures, when a sacrifice is made, it is . . . a gift or a bribe to the deity that is being invited to do something for us or give us something. But when a figure is sacrificed in the planting cultures, that figure itself is the god. The person who dies is buried and becomes the food.[7]

The idea of sacrifice comes up over and over again throughout the Futhark—which only makes sense, as we have the runes because of Odin's personal sacrifice of himself to himself. Uruz is the sacrifice of the creature who gives their life for us, but Uruz is also a rune of the hunt. What can you give up in order to go after what you truly desire? What is holding you back and how can you break free from it? Sometimes sacrifice is a great honor and sometimes you should hold fast and not compromise—this rune can help you determine whether sacrifice or holding steady is more important.

The more you work with the runes, the more you'll discover ways that they reference one another. I've already talked about how Uruz and Fehu are related, but it's important to find relationships between all of the runes. For example, you know that Uruz may have these "hunter" qualities when paired with Eiwaz—the hunter's bow. Finding pairs, similarities, and other facets of the runes will help you to unlock different meanings in them.

This is a natural rune to call upon to bring more and greater energy to your magical workings. If you aren't feeling confident, but you know that you need to put energy and force behind your magic, chant Uruz three times in circle. Call upon or carry Uruz with you anytime you need to go into negotiations, when you need courage to have a difficult conversation, or when you need to stick up for yourself. You can also use Uruz when you need to smash through barriers. The aurochs is not a creature that is held; Auðhumla may have a beatific nature about her, but she is certainly not a pushover. She is not kept, she creates on her

---

7 Campbell, *The Power of Myth.*

own terms. But with creation also comes the power of destruction. Uruz gives us the strength to have our own convictions—and fight for them.

Rune	Transliteration	International Phonetic Alphabet	Proto-Germanic Name	Meaning
ᚢ	u	/u(:)/	Uruz	aurochs (or sleet)

ANGLO-SAXON RUNE POEM:

> The aurochs is proud and has great horns;
> it is a very savage beast and fights with its horns;
> a great ranger of the moors, it is a creature of mettle.

ICELANDIC RUNE POEM:

> Shower
> lamentation of the clouds
> and ruin of the hay-harvest
> and abomination of the shepherd.

NORWEGIAN RUNE POEM

> Dross comes from bad iron;
> the reindeer often races over the frozen snow.

Opportunities for Ancestral Discovery

Fehu and Uruz together represent large, cloven-hoofed animals, but one is domesticated and one is wild. The cow lives within the confines of the farm, and the aurochs lives on the outskirts. Between them is the fence or the hedgerow, which was considered an in-between or liminal place. How do your wild and tamed natures come together?

The Norse divided their year into two parts: Summer and Winter. Summer is when everything needed to be grown and divided between families, and then the winters were long and harsh. Great care was taken to make sure there was enough to last the winter. And yet, as we know from folklore, people did still hunt in the winter. Meditate on this idea of Summer being Abundance + Harvest, and the Winter being the Hunt.

RADICAL URUZ

- What aspects of Uruz do you identify with the most? What about Uruz is difficult for you to process?

- What is your greatest strength? How can you use this strength in your activism to make necessary change in the world?

- What nourishment do you need to fuel your strength?

THURS/THURISAZ

Keywords: conflict, choice, aggression, weapon, giants

Thurisaz is the introduction of conflict and aggression into the rune cycle. It represents alternatively giants and thorns. "Thorn" is actually the word that is used to describe this letter when going through the Futhark, and it is still used in Scandinavian languages today. Thurisaz represents a pretty harsh but necessary awakening. One thing to bear in mind is that this rune can also be used for protection, and on a deeper level it represents the *need* to protect yourself.

The more dramatic meaning of this rune is "giant." The giants in Norse mythology are powerful beings who often stand in opposition to the gods. They are forces of nature, quite literally. They are also connected to our deepest impulses and instincts. Kari Tauring refers to Thurisaz as the connection with our deepest, animal brains[8]—it can act as a bridge between our modern brain and our instinctual brain. It is what gets us to run, or to fight, when we need to.

I know that my Nordic ancestors—especially those living in the harsher climates of northern Norway and Iceland—organized their homes and farms for the greatest level of protection. Farms were organized into the Ingard (the inner layer, where the family resided) and the Utgard (the outer layer, beyond the first fence but still an area the family would have known).[9] You went hunting in the Utgard, but you raised cattle and sheep in the Ingard. On a metaphysical level the Ingard represented the layer of protection. You would be looked after and kept safe if you were within the Ingard. The Utgard is where you needed to be on your toes—to be able to defend yourself from harm. This rune is our first introduction to

---

8   Tauring, *The Runes.*
9   Tauring, "Frith and Grith."

the Utgard. It's like the famous line from *Game of Thrones*: "Oh, my sweet summer child."

Thurisaz is deeply connected to Thor—even linguistically. Of course Thurisaz is connected to Thor! Even if we think about this rune on a simple, etymological level, the sounds of the rune are connected to Thor. Thurisaz—Thor—Thurses. Thor is many things—god of strength, protector of the Aesir, as well as the weather god, most notably god of thunder. Many of us first got to know Thor from the Marvel comics (which are in no way intended to be a faithful retelling—but they are fun). We think of him first and foremost as a warrior, a protector. But the agrarian aspect of Thor is really important to keep in mind: Thor was worshipped largely by farmers, and you can see it in the folk charms that were passed down through the generations.[10] It makes sense: if you're a largely agrarian society, the weather makes or breaks you. Pray to the god of thunder to bring rain that will nourish your crops, rather than harm them. Pray that you will not be obliterated by hail; pray that you will get enough snow over the winter to create a solid water table for the summer. Thor in all aspects lives up to his kenning "Friend of Man."[11]

There is an added layer to the protection Thor offers. Thor has a great strength and is famously the only one who knows how to wield it. Thor carries Mjölnir, which you can see as a sort of extension of his strength and mythic powers. The gods are also very protective of Mjölnir—they know that if Thor's powers were in anyone else's hands, it would be disastrous. The real power of Thor is in his ability to both control and console nature—and indeed, his primary goal in the mythos is to protect his mother Jörð (Earth) from attacking forces from the Utgard.[12] He is an intermediary between people and the forces of chaos. Thor balances the chaos of the giants, but doesn't totally obliterate them. He keeps it in the Utgard.

Thurisaz also resembles Mjölnir in shape, and so it is not just a representation of Thor but of the primary weapon he uses to protect his

---

10 Gårdbäck, *Trolldom.*
11 Smith, *The Way of Fire and Ice.*
12 Kvilhaug, *The Seed of Yggdrasil.*

loved ones. Mjölnir has many magical purposes, but its starring role is the primary weapon the gods could use against the giants. The Jotun were the primary enemies of the Aesir (after their war with the Vanir was settled).[13] But Thor's name means giant and Mjölnir means lightning—he is literally a god who wields lightning as protection.[14] Thurisaz is inextricably connected to not just Thor, but the jotun themselves. If the gods represent order, the jotun represent chaos. Kvilhaug talks about Thor as being the force that can control the chaos[15]—and for me Thurisaz is the rune that is most helpful in that control.

Thor is the gateway between the Ingard—where you are safe—and the Utgard. Thurisaz interacts with and combats chaos on both an internal and external level—it is an advanced energy that the experienced sorcerer can use in shadow work and setting boundaries.

Thurisaz would be an incredibly helpful rune to call when you are drawing boundaries with an abuser. When I've had to draw those boundaries in the past, I've had to do it multiple times. They don't believe me the first time, or come out of the woodwork right when I'm doing better. Drawing upon the protection of Thurisaz during this boundary work would sting. Use Thurisaz to draw protective magic around yourself, to disrupt the patterns of abuse. Then, after you've had the conversation and drawn your boundary with your abuser, and they try to come back . . . they'll feel that force. Thurisaz is active defense—and it would return the toxicity to your abuser, while at the same time protecting you.

When they get a taste of that energy pushed back at them, they will be far less likely to disrespect your boundaries again.

This is an example of using Thurisaz in your own life on a small scale.

My question is, how can we work with Thurisaz through the lens of anti-oppression?

The protection magic of Thurisaz works on multiple levels. Not only does it help to create boundaries between yourself and your enemies,

---

13 Lafayllve, *A Practical Heathen's Guide.*
14 Kvilhaug, *The Seed of Yggdrasil.*
15 Kvilhaug.

but you can also use it internally. In my experience, Thurisaz the thorn can also be used to pull evil out of the spirit body. You can perform an energetically complex cutaway ritual and use the Thurisaz rune to draw toxicity away from the spirit body. This process is either internal or external—one that you do on yourself or one that you do with your most trusted coven members. And drawing toxicity out of your spirit self? Well. That is both personal and collective liberation.

I have a theory that you could use Thurisaz to draw toxic messages inherited from the overculture out of your subconscious. This rune is perfect for shadow-working your negative beliefs, habits, all of those things that are unhealthy that have been passed down to you through ørlog or other means. You can isolate and begin to extract toxic messages about your body, the impacts of toxic masculinity, limiting beliefs, and also examine your own privileges.

For me, it makes sense to work with Thurisaz to examine my white privilege.

Being white means that I need to interrogate the ways that racism and white privilege have been imprinted in my life. I grew up in a household that believed in racial equality and class justice, with two strongly feminist parents, but there are still messages that I take in every day from the overculture, messages that seep into my unconscious. I know what my values are: equity and justice for all. But a part of living up to these values is also understanding when I need to break the patterns of toxic whiteness that I've learned all my life.

White privilege has an impact on you no matter your intellectual understanding of equity, no matter how much you value racial justice. I've been thinking about a sort of psychic extraction process—to be able to look at the different parts of myself and magically reject those pieces that don't mesh with my values. Thurisaz as thorn can help to pull out these things. It gets under your skin, and as you extract the thorn, more comes with it.

Rune	Transliteration	International Phonetic Alphabet	Proto-Germanic Name	Meaning
Þ	Þ | th	/θ/, /ð/	Thurisaz	giant, thorn

ANGLO-SAXON RUNE POEM:

The thorn is exceedingly sharp,
an evil thing for any knight to touch,
uncommonly severe on all who sit among them.

ICELANDIC RUNE POEM:

Giant
torture of women
and cliff-dweller
and husband of a giantess.

NORWEGIAN RUNE POEM:

Giant causes anguish to women; misfortune makes few men cheerful.

Opportunities for Ancestral Discovery

Think about the different natural landscapes your ancestors lived in. What might they have needed protection from in these places? How does that connect to what you need protection from?

Thurisaz can help us connect to our primal, instinctual mind. Think about times when your own instincts have taken over. What surprised you? Were there things that felt like they came from a deep, ancestral connection? How might your ancestral history have influenced you?

RADICAL THURISAZ

- Some occultists have associated Thurisaz with the planet Saturn. How does this shift your perspective of this rune?

- Thurisaz both recognizes chaos and helps us to set boundaries with our own chaos. Take a moment to journal about your chaos. How do you work both with and against this inner storm?

- Anger is sacred, but we don't let ourselves fully feel that anger much. We have to keep it penned in, productive. What anger have you deferred? How can you set things right with yourself by feeling that anger? What would it look like to honor *all* emotions—not just the orderly ones?

ANSUZ

Keywords: Odin, mouth, breath, deity, connection, communication

Ansuz represents the breath, connection to a deity, and communication. It the first thought, first word. There is a certain level of hope that comes with Ansuz that feels like a breath of fresh air after the last rune we discussed. The second vowel sound in the Futhark, Ansuz is ecstasy over finally making the words work. It is that clever turn of phrase that worms its way into your head. It's the sudden flash of inspiration, the wild trance babble that spills from you in the middle of ritual.

In Norse cosmology Odin (Vod) and his brothers Vili and Vé each breathe life into the first humans after slaying Ymir. They end the rule of primordial chaos over the world, and from Ymir's body they build the nine worlds. They later create humanity out of ash and elm trees. Vili's gift is Willpower, Vé's gift is Holiness, and Vod's gift is Spirit itself. This spirit is imparted through breath, and it is through speech that both holiness and will are conveyed. One thing that is specific to Norse heathenry is the emphasis on the spoken word. There are examples of magical incantations and chanting in most cultures—including speaking in tongues in certain Christian sects. There is great emphasis on speaking in Norse practice.

Ansuz channels sacred poetry, raises your energy in circle, and allows you to bring forward messages from the unconscious.

For me, ritual is always ... noisy. I don't know if this is true for other heathens, but there is always a lot of chanting and incantations for me. Stream-of-consciousness speaking helps me to get to the heart of the matter. I talk my way around the meaning, and then my mind starts to narrow. I invoke Ansuz, and the proper incantation comes to me. The words, the tense, the timing, all of it comes to my mouth as if risen from a well.

One of the things I work on the most often with my own teacher in Norse heathenry is impeccability of word. This is incredibly important within Norse practice. The *Hávamál* is filled with verses about how important it is to mind your word and make sure that you are speaking the truth.[16] The Norse texts emphasize deep thought before you speak. Odin is just spiteful enough to make your foolish wishes come true. If you don't take time to really think them through and figure out what you really want, you might be in trouble later. Reading the old manners guide that is "Sayings of the High One," you can really see how the stereotype of the stoic Norseman was birthed. There was always a middle ground between promising too much and saying too little. It's a difficult balance to strike.

Ansuz then represents two things above all: a connection to Odin and your personal guiding spirits, as well as communication of ideas. Ansuz is the rune of speech, of poetry, of focus and communication, and can even help us tap into the primary messages we need to learn and share in our own lifetimes.[17] This is the rune to call in when you are suffering from writer's block or inability to focus. When this rune comes up, it is often urging us to go further in our intellectual and spiritual courses. It is an expansion of ideas, with the knowledge that our ideas are in alignment with our own highest good. So we move forward, pressing harder. Things bend and move easily, as the path is laid clear.

Ansuz transforms our experiences from nameless things to stories we can tell. It puts words to actions and translates the meaning behind what we do into a language that can be shared. Which brings me to another meaning of Ansuz: deity.

It is damn near impossible to study the runes without also studying Odin. He is the god that brought the runes to earth, that has translated their meaning. Odin has many names. In Anglo-Saxon he is known as Woden, Old Saxon as Wodan, and in Old High German as Wuotan or Wotan. Odin is not the first being and is not the creator of the world. But he is the leader of the Aesir, the tribe of gods that, in Norse mythology, won sovereignty after warring with the Vanir and the Giants. Odin comes in many forms, but is often known as the wanderer. Throughout

16 Larrington, *The Poetic Edda.*
17 Mountfort, *Nordic Runes.*

mythology he is depicted as wearing a wide-brimmed hat, cloaked, with a long beard. The film design for Gandalf the Grey could easily have been lifted from Norse mythology.

The story is that Odin knew there was a deeper magic, one that he didn't know how to use. But there were beings older and wiser than Odin—the three Norns, who lived at the center of Yggdrasil, the world tree. The Norns represented Fate; they knew everything that would ever happen. When Odin came to them, they said he needed to make a sacrifice. He gave up an eye. He hung upon the great tree Yggdrasil for nine days and nine nights. And on that last night, as dawn broke, the runes came to him. They floated out of Mímir's well, the well of wyrd, and he was struck with a sudden inspiration and understanding.[18]

Odin carried these secrets with him. He spoke of some secrets in Asgard, but kept others to himself. That is why each heathen must find their own relationship to each of the runes. They reveal their mysteries to you slowly, steadily, over time. You need to develop your own relationship with these energies, and a part of that means that you will become a conspirator with the runes themselves. They will teach you to keep their secrets.

Odin is the god of wisdom and logic. If Freyja is about wild instinct and mysteries, Odin is about translating the awe of those mysteries into a language we can understand. Communication and mental faculties are deeply important for this god. In my personal relationship with him he has been incredibly helpful for long-term research and study projects. Two of his familiars, the ravens Huginn and Muninn, are representations of "Thought" and "Memory" in our soul bodies. We each have a Huginn and Muninn that we carry with us—they are literally parts of our souls in Norse cosmology.[19] The Norse soul is not the same as the soul that we think of in modern culture: the Nordic soul is divided into at least four distinct parts, which is very different from the body-mind duality or even the mind-body-soul system.[20] There are distinct parts of the soul, many of which will come up over the course of our rune study.

---

18 Larrington, *The Poetic Edda.*
19 Tauring, "Soul Parts and Healing."
20 Smith, *Spinning Wyrd.*

But Norse cosmology also works with other teachers. Ansuz is not just about clarity of thought and memory, but it is expressing those things beautifully. This is not just a rune of Odin, but also of Odin's son Baldr. It recently struck me that it's strange that I don't see terribly many people working with Baldr. He is one of the most beautiful of the deities. Baldr goes through an underworld journey, and in spite of wide grieving from the gods, he is released by Hel only when it is time to create a new world after Ragnarök.[21]

As queer readers, then, we see the necessity of learning to use words to break through to the real truth. Ansuz rises up above it all and shows us that core of truth, so we can better articulate it. Ansuz is using they/them or neopronouns even though that is more difficult for other people, in speaking your truth, in standing behind the truth of our trans queer relatives. It is using words to eviscerate our enemies, to assert our existence and our rightness.

Rune	Transliteration	International Phonetic Alphabet	Proto-Germanic Name	Meaning
ᚠ	a	/a(:)/	Ansuz	"god," "breath," speech

ANGLO-SAXON RUNE POEM:

The mouth is the source of all language,
a pillar of wisdom and a comfort to wise men,
a blessing and a joy to every knight.

ICELANDIC RUNE POEM:

God
aged Gautr
and prince of Asgard
and lord of Valhalla.

---

21 Larrington, *The Poetic Edda.*

NORWEGIAN RUNE POEM:

Estuary is the way of most journeys;
but a scabbard is of swords.

Opportunities for Ancestral Discovery

How does your family view divinity or god? How does that sit with you—does it feel okay, or is there something complicated there? Write about what you have learned about gods from your family, what makes sense to you, and where you differ.

RADICAL ANSUZ

- Thurisaz and Ansuz together can be a powerful working of boundaries: defending yourself with the strength of Thurisaz, and then communicating those boundaries to others. How might a meditation on these two runes help you create better boundaries in your life?

- Freewrite for five minutes. Don't allow your pen or pencil to leave the page, just write stream-of-conscious whatever comes into your head. Unlock your subconscious and bring it into the conscious realm. What has come out? Are there any sentences that feel like a truth?

- What does purposeful speech mean to you? How can you be more dedicated to speaking the truth, and speaking carefully?

RAIDHO

Keywords: riding, chariot, travel, fylgja, transition

Travel was of course extremely important in both pre-Viking and Viking culture. There's even a verse in the *Hávamál* that states that you are supposed to go and travel widely, to learn the wisdom of other lands and learn from the culture of other people. I think often of the idea of a "quest," something that you would undertake to gain specific knowledge. It's the Hero's Journey all over again. But Raidho also reminds us that our quests can be internal. We can work to expand our mind and soul beyond their current existence, beyond the parameters that our own lives have set. It is not just about travel but also about momentum.

We also need to think about Raidho as helping us to move forward in many areas of our lives: in our careers, on our spiritual paths, and toward greater health. There is no one way to read the rune, and no one area in your life that it can show up. I often read Raidho as a bit of an amplifying rune for this reason: it highlights where you're ready to expand, move forward, and explore. When this rune shows up it's telling you to get going and take action. Stop thinking about it, and start doing it. There's something very hopeful about this rune—it truly is exploratory.

This is a rune of change, yes, but it is also a rune of accepting the change that is necessary.

It represents the way forward. it's far more likely that you're at the beginning of a certain path than at the end of it. Tauring refers to this rune as the journeyman's rune: It's all about the wisdom that is gathered on the road.[22] I also like to think of this rune as being integral to creativity for these reasons. If it is the journeyman's rune, then it is a musician on tour—not the process of writing the music. Whether you're

---

22 Tauring, *The Runes.*

starting out on something totally new or deepening your own expertise, you can bet that this is a rune that will open your eyes to new ways of doing things. There is always something new to learn. It demands action, rather than waiting for the action and inspiration to come to you. It's a rune in movement.

Raidho represents the act of riding—whether on a horse or in a chariot, this rune shows that you are going places. This is the first "constructed" rune of the Elder Futhark.[23] It's not another living creature or concept: it can quite literally mean the wagon, the wheel, the cart. This feels important to note, because there are so many human-constructed things that might have showed up first (house, clothing, books, and so forth). The fact that the first constructed thing in the Elder Futhark is the cart/chariot/wagon shows the importance that the Norse and Germanic peoples placed on travel. Many contemporary rune workers view this rune as a representation of the act of traveling.[24]

Raidho then feels really active. Here is the story of the Futhark so far: we've firmly established our home base, our strength, our boundaries, and connected with Spirit, and now we can take those ideas and spread them from the road. We can set out and explore, learn more, and adapt where we need to. In the *Flateyjarbók* (an important Icelandic medieval manuscript), we learn that once a year, Freyr was carried around in a wagon through southern Sweden as a way of blessing the fields and praying for a good agricultural season.[25] This was a herald of the changing of the year, of bounty, and of the necessity of traveling between communities. The chariot in Norse culture is also associated with the goddess Sunna, who drives the sun across the sky in a chariot. There are victory, brightness, and triumph to this rune. The winter is long, and harsh, and dark, and so most imagery related to the sun and light becomes triumphant. When Raidho shows up, it often signifies that you are indeed on the right path and that you are able to move forward quickly.

23 Tauring, *The Runes.*
24 Mountfort, *Nordic Runes.*
25 Turville-Petre, *Myth and Religion of the North.*

Raidho recognizes the power that our allies have on our movements. Because this rune made it into the Younger Futhark, we have more rune poems to help us understand the context of this rune. The Icelandic rune poem reads: "Joy of the horsemen, and speedy journey, and toil of the steed."[26] In fact, the labor of the horse is often honored in the rune poems. The Norwegian rune poem states that "Riding is said to be the worst thing for horses; Reginn forged the finest sword."[27] There's an empathy here, a connection between the rider and the horse, the driver and the vehicle. This also shows a certain cognition on the part of the vehicle, an understanding that the rider must be grateful to the horse for their willingness to carry us forward on the journey. Where the Chariot tarot card implies a sort of victory, a sort of control over the vehicle, Raidho recognizes the impact of partnership with the vehicle. There is a sense that Raidho takes you deeper, but only when you're ready. Raidho is not the comfortable temptation to stay in your tidy, beautiful chariot: Raidho is the vehicle you go to when you're ready to accept your own path of destiny.

I am not one for destiny; I am a firm believer in will and self-determination. However, I do think there are lessons that we are meant to engage with in our lives. They come in many forms, and Raidho can lead the way. It can act as a bit of a compass.

Sometimes, of course, Raidho signifies not just movement in external parts of your life, but also internal, spiritual exploration. Trollreid (troll-ridden) and Gandreid (witch-ride) are two words in Old Norse that mean to be ridden by spiritual forces and have -reid as a suffix.[28] Because of this, many esoteric runeworkers use Raidho as a rune to begin journeying in the spirit realm. And it's not just other spirits riding us; it is also getting to know other aspects of our souls.

The Norse believed in multiple soul parts that would come to your aid during spirit travel. There are soul parts that are not bound by your flesh and blood—they are able to travel throughout the dream world. And of all these parts of the body, Raidho is most closely related to

26 "Rune Poems," Wikisource.
27 "Rune Poems."
28 Zoëga, *A Concise Dictionary.*

the fylgja. They are a personal guiding spirit connected to you. In many other European traditions this figure is referred to as a fetch, so if you've seen the term "fetch" around, you've already got some context for this soul part.[29] Oftentimes, the fylgja is an animal form, but it doesn't have to be. The idea is that the fylgja moves through the world in a way that is different from your physical body. They are not the same as a familiar spirit or guardian spirit because they are a part of your soul. They are personally interested and invested in you and your growth, and are here to guide you. We inherit our fylgja from our ancestors.[30] Each person has their own fylgja, and the form the follower takes is connected to that person's character. A noble person might have a horse or a bear, a cunning or intuitive person might have a raven, a trickster might have a fox or coyote.

When you have a relationship with this spirit, it is able to help you in ways that straddle the spirit and physical realms. They can act as a sort of familiar, navigating your dreams, delivering messages on the astral plane. There are tales of a spiritual person being able to send their fylgja to appear in a friend's dreams to deliver messages. Sometimes, when you are about to meet someone new, your fylgja will appear in their dreams the night before, to ensure that this will be a good working relationship. They can also serve as protectors, steering negative people away from you subtly on the astral plane. The fylgja will do this throughout your life, and if you cultivate a relationship with them, you will become more aware of their workings in the world and you will be able to work with them in your magic.

Because the runes help us find the language we need to understand these greater forces, Raidho is the perfect rune to connect to your fylgja. Carry Raidho with you during a meditation; visualize Raidho as a bright light, guiding you further. If you are attempting to meet your fylgja but there are many spirit forms, use Raidho to point you toward the correct being.

---

29 Smith, *Spinning Wyrd.*.
30 Tauring, "Soul Parts and Healing."

If you want to engage with the fylgja, that is a very personal journey. Spend time at your altar; open yourself up in meditation to the spirit body. Once you have made contact, and you know the form your guide takes, you can leave them offerings on your altar. If my fylgja is a raven, I would leave them nuts and seeds. If my fylgja is a fox, I might leave them dried meats and fruit. They are a spirit that is a part of you—honor them as you honor the gods, and honor yourself.

Of course, journeying in the spirit realm is not for everyone. Merely understanding the runes does not mean that you will be ready for journeying in the spirit world. In fact, to be "hag-ridden" often means that you are bewitched in some way, that there is even potentially a plague of spirits chasing you. When students ask about the otherworld, I am open with what I know, but I also know that the spirit world changes for each one of us based on our experiences. In general, if you don't feel ready for this kind of work, that's okay. Focus instead on meditation.

The runes can help us to ground ourselves as we go on these spirit quests.

Contemporary Norse spirit traveling often features Raidho and Ingwaz as gateway runes to the spirit realm. Chant Raidho and visualize the rune as you enter your trance states to connect with the spirit realm and with your soul parts. But Raidho is about more than travel in the spirit realm—it is also about the transition between states of being in the physical realm. This makes the rune a beautiful assistant for trans heathens. It is a rune of transformation. Raidho can help you figure out what it is you want, and how to get there. My trans friends who transition physically often take a long time to sort through what it is that they want in their transition. Raidho can help with this by providing support and courage.

May Raidho help you to manifest your sacred goals.

Rune	Transliteration	International Phonetic Alphabet	Proto-Germanic Name	Meaning
R	r	/r/	Raidho	ride, journey

ANGLO-SAXON RUNE POEM:

*Riding seems easy to every warrior while he is indoors
and very courageous to him who traverses the high-roads
on the back of a stout horse.*

ICELANDIC RUNE POEM:

*Riding
joy of the horsemen
and speedy journey
and toil of the steed.*

NORWEGIAN RUNE POEM:

*Riding is said to be the worst thing for horses;
Reginn forged the finest sword.*

Opportunities for Ancestral Discovery

Think about all the ways your ancestors may have traveled. Migration and movements of people are a really important theme in our ancestral lineage, and they can also be very loaded, so be gentle with yourself for this.

What kind of spiritual assistance would your own ancestors have used when traveling?

QUEER RAIDHO

- Think back to a time when you were really making headway, when it felt like you were breaking through barriers and making things happen. How did that feel in your body?

- If you're a tarot reader, pull out the Chariot card as well as the Raidho rune and place them next to each other. Get yourself into a meditative headspace. How does the energy of Raidho feel? How does the energy of the Chariot feel? Write down any similarities or differences.

- What areas of your life do you need to take action in? How can you channel the energy of Raidho to take that action?

KAUNAZ /KENAZ

Keywords: fire, ideas, spark of life, ulcer

While the fire can warm the home and light up dark nights, it can also burn your cozy house to the ground. If the flame is too weak, it won't produce enough warmth, but if it is too great, it can destroy all in its path. Kaunaz is all of these things at once.

Kaunaz is also directly linked to knowledge and truth. When we say something "came to light," we are inadvertently making that connection between fire, light, and truth.

Kaunaz is also the spread of inspiration and ideas between people and places.

> *Brand from brand kindles until it's burned*
> *Spark kindles from spark,*
> *Man becomes wise by speaking to men,*
> *But gets dull, staying dumb.*
>
> (*Hávamál:* 57)

Fire is necessary. Fire is destructive. Fire is cleansing.

As the forest and the prairie need regular fires to clean out the old growth and make way for new, so does the fire of truth need to purge, purge, purge. Kaunaz is both truth and mystery—the process of death for regeneration. I keep hoping that as the truth comes out we will see a change in the trajectory. But there is so much that needs to be illuminated, and so much that needs death. What we need is the transformative fire of the funeral pyre—that transmutation, between states, to make room for new growth. The only thing that gives me hope is the sense that these times are the final death throes of the old, unjust ways—that this is the desperate clawing of a society trying to maintain relevance in the face of climate disaster.

I've been thinking of holy rage lately. The world seems to be on fire. There is an overwhelming sense of hopelessness. I've been thinking of holy rage lately. The world seems to be on fire. There is an overwhelming sense of hopelessness. We are fighting to protect our human rights. People are still being held in cages at the border. Journalists, aid workers, and civilians are dying in foreign wars. These are all things that desperately need to change.

Kaunaz at Ragnarök is not gentle illumination of pretty poems and truisms. It is the consuming fire that will take it all down, for even the gods are corrupt. Kaunaz is the fire that burns down the facade, leaving behind truth. Kaunaz is the light in the darkness, the ace in the hole, the pawn about to check the king. Kaunaz is the light of truth that shines when journalists take on corrupt politics. Kaunaz is the fire that spits from the mouth of the human rights lawyer winning case after case for their immigrant clients.

Use the energy of Kaunaz in these times to find the inner strength necessary to resist, to revolt.

There is a connection between the element of fire and memory of our ancestors. There are many recorded burial rites of the Norse, but cremation stands out. Whether burned in effigy, a corpse burned on a pyre, or setting their ship aflame, fire played a role in the funerary rites of ancient Nordic people. Fire initiates the transition of the dead to the spirit realm, and many believe that it was a fire ritual that initiated the new king or the new spiritual leader to their role. Kaunaz is the mystery of regeneration through death or sacrifice. Kaunaz and Nauthiz both represent necessary communication with and honoring of our ancestors. The funeral pyre is a gateway for the soul, a way to release the soul from the trappings of its body and into the spirit realm. This release of the spirit is necessary for it to be born again in a new form.

But the funeral pyre isn't only for the dead: it is also a necessary witness for the living.

Through the funerary service we are able to release our own attachments to our dead loved ones. We see them transform before our eyes into ash. There is no body that could be reanimated and come back in our loved one's old form—it is a complete release from the physical form their soul used in the lifetime we knew them.

And still it's a cycle.

Kaunaz is not only the fire that keeps us warm, it is also what creates a home for us.

In many magical and occult traditions, you should draw a circle to create sacred space. In Wicca, this looks like cleansing and charging the space, calling the corners, calling the gods and goddesses. In other traditions this looks like burning sage, burning incense. Many traditions use fire as a marker of sacred space. I know that I've never really had an altar that didn't feature a candle in the center. Many who follow the Norse path will carry a candle throughout the home to cleanse the space, to protect the space, to cast a protective "circle." Kaunaz is a rune representing all of this—it is our generative relationship with fire.

Magical circle also creates spaces of truth. It creates spaces designated for speaking with your gods, spaces for self-reflection, spaces for finding your spiritual truth. It also helps us to find truth in fiction. Kaunaz is the alchemist of your mind space—transforming energy to something higher. It makes sense that Kaunaz can also serve as one way to transition between the realms of life and death. The runes also help us to communicate knowledge from within. Kaunaz is concerned not only with the fire but also with the stories told around the fire. This is one of the primary differences between Kaunaz and Nauthiz—the other fire rune.

Kaunaz creates sacred spaces; it blesses the liminal with its light. Kaunaz brings us truth and shows us the way into new ways of life. When we apply Kaunaz to our lives, it offers a consistent space and forgiveness for transformation and experimentation. This is the second part of reincarnation—the re-homing of the soul into a new body. This is especially sacred for trans heathens: Kaunaz helps us rebirth ourselves. Especially when combined with a rune like Ingwaz or Eiwaz, this is a great indication of support for transition. This comes from the human urge to continue to grow, to change, to keep the collective story of humanity moving forward.

But Kaunaz has another meaning that people don't talk about as often: ulcer, boil, or scab.

Most esoteric rune workers use the Anglo-Saxon meaning of the rune (fire) rather than the ulcer (Norwegian plus Icelandic). It's a little more encouraging, and it makes more sense if we're using the runes to work through some personal expansion stuff. It also makes sense in terms of the progression of the Futhark up until this point—you need that extra fire to keep your chariot moving forward, to follow through on the ideas you've sparked. But I will also talk about the healing power of the ulcer image.

The ulcer is the pain of creativity not fulfilled, of ideas shelved and set aside. So often we associate ulcers with stress, with being overworked and not having access to the right kind of nourishment, or both. In Chinese medicine, ulcers are seen as being caused by excess heat in the body. So there is still friction here, but it is stymied. This can also be an indicator that there is something you need to exorcise: Kaunaz then encourages you get it out, before it becomes an issue.

I also want to take a moment to do a quick comparison between the two Fire runes: Kaunaz and Nauthiz. Fire is an extremely important element in Nordic culture because our mythology starts with the clash of fire and ice. It is out of this clash that the world is born. Therefore, we should pay special attention to runes that represent fire or ice in our readings. Kaunaz and Nauthiz show two different sides of this element.

Kaunaz is the fire rune that works most closely with the creative aspect of fire. When I think of the first fire, I think of Kaunaz before I think of Nauthiz.

Where Kaunaz is generative, with the power to overtake and consume, Nauthiz represents need. We approach these fires at very different times, and they both have the power to burn beyond our control. You can think about them both working together to create balance within this element: Kaunaz, creation; Nauthiz, need. Kaunaz is the creativity necessary to develop our communities, and as it works with Nauthiz, we learn how to creatively meet our needs.

Rune	Transliteration	International Phonetic Alphabet	Proto-Germanic Name	Meaning
ᚲ	k(c)	/k/	Kaunan, kaunaz	ulcer, torch

ANGLO-SAXON RUNE POEM:

The torch is known to every living man by its pale, bright flame;
it always burns where princes sit within.

ICELANDIC RUNE POEM:

Ulcer
disease fatal to children
and painful spot
and abode of mortification.

NORWEGIAN RUNE POEM:

Ulcer is fatal to children;
death makes a corpse pale.

Opportunities for Ancestral Discovery

Are there any ways that your ancestors traditionally lit their homes? I'm thinking things like specific fireplaces, or a kind of oil lamp, or specific candle-making techniques. If possible, recreate something like this in your homes.

Build a bonfire. As you sit, stare into the flames, and chant Kaunaz to yourself. Imagine that you are inviting your well ancestors to the fire. Listen and see what they want to share with you.

RADICAL KAUNAZ

- What inspires you? Journal about your inspiration, make a vision board, make some lists. Find ways to bring these forces of inspiration into your daily life more regularly.

- What are some things that need to burn, to be sacrificed in order to create something new? Write through them here.

- Kaunaz represents our will to create, to make our way through projects. But what if you ignore your projects? What if you ignore this inspiration? In other words—what's at stake for you?

GYFU/GEBO

Keywords: gift, reciprocity, mutual aid, thriving

Gyfu is one of my favorite runes because it is in this rune where we can start to crack open and get to the soft underbelly of heathenry.

The cultural obsession with the "Viking aesthetic" makes the Norse pantheon appear particularly brutal. Vikings were brutal conquerors who sacked cities, whose reputation as violent barbarians preceded them. But the Vikings, the ones who went raiding, were a minority of the population, and the Viking age lasted only around four hundred years. The vast majority of heathens did not go Viking, but rather tended their farms in this period. Throughout the Eddas are reflections on ethics and morals, what is "right" and what is "wrong." Yes, the world of the Norse was brutal, but every culture and people around the world have periods of difficulty and even brutality. In Norse literature there are stanzas and stanzas about proper behavior, about being conscious of others' needs, about the importance of social gestures.

On our journey so far, we have focused on communication, abundance, protection—all things that work on a very personal level. Gyfu is the first rune that really talks about how to act in community. This rune breaks us outside of ourselves and helps us to see how to show up. It is the rune of the gift. Reciprocity and mutual aid played an essential role in the Norse world. The *Hávamál* is filled with stanzas about the proper etiquette of gift-giving, a sign of just how essential gifting was to the culture.[31] Gyfu teaches us that we need to be generous with what we have, but that we also need to get our own needs met first.

In these old times the ancestors learned to treat strangers as if they were the gods, because they just might be a god in disguise. The Eddas

---

31 "Hávamál," in Larrington, *The Poetic Edda.*

teach that wealth is not to be hoarded—rather, it is meant to be shared. There were even laws governing hospitality. Lafayllve shares that "warrior cultures tend to prioritize hospitality in general, and once under a host's roof, a guest expects not just to be taken care of, but to be protected."[32]

First, let's talk about the rune itself. In a reading, Gyfu can refer to contracts, agreements, alliances, as well as gifts and endowments. There were laws governing gifts that if you received a gift, you would need to give something to the gifter. I have also heard stories of heathens misappropriating this as a sort of "eye for an eye" edict—that they will demand specific things from their hosts, and will keep track of who has given what. This is a capitalist rewriting of the rune itself, a modernization that doesn't sit well with the spirit of Gyfu. This rune is actually about the reciprocity of gifts—it is a covenant, the understanding that if I receive a gift, I will give it forward. In a way, Gyfu acts as an oath. It means that when the person who gave you something needs something, you need to give something to them when they are in need. This is grandmothers borrowing eggs from one another to bake bread, it is not a hoard of gifts given at Christmastime.

Gyfu instructs us on how to use the gifts we are given for the greater good. This is how Gyfu represents not just gift giving, but also social contracts that we make with one another for the better of the community. There is perhaps some sacrifice in the gift-giving, but nothing more than you can afford to lose. Gyfu represents a voluntary sacrifice of wealth, resources, and time to whatever you hold sacred. So often, that includes our communities—so make sure you are giving back!

Another important lesson of Gyfu is learning to receive with grace. This is often very difficult for people, particularly when you have trauma around money or other baggage about money and worth. Gyfu asks you to soften, to recognize your inherent worth. When people give you something, it is a sign of love. They want you to have what you need. The understanding in rune work is that when you have what you need, you will help to provide for the people around you.

---

32 Lafayllve, *A Practical Heathen's Guide.*

Both giving and receiving with grace are essential aspects of the queer experience. When family abandons us, we need to find networks of our own support. Gyfu shows up in this way—it helps us and holds us as we build new structures. Learning how to ask for what we want can be so difficult, especially if what we want—how we want—has been denied us for so long. Gyfu is a balm, a healing rune that tells us our desires are valid. Gyfu reminds us that we all have gifts to share.

Heathenry has a huge emphasis on ancestor work. We inherit the legacies of our ancestors, we inherit their ørlog, but our lives are also built around the choices we make. While we may start in an unequal position, throughout our lives we are in constant exchange—of resources, trade, time, love, community. A gift received demands a gift given. A gift is an oath to that person—a signal that yes, you are on the right path. I respect you. And I also know that we are in this together, as one society. In the Norse tradition, you do not get a gift without giving a gift. If you are not generous with the gifts you've been given, whether they be mundane or divine, you are considered immoral.

We all do better when we all do better—so give of your own resources freely.

It is necessary, when worshipping your ancestors or the Norse gods, to leave them offerings. I've done this in many ways. It can be a shot glass of wine that I keep on my altar and refresh every day. It can be setting aside the bones from your meat—the gods and spirits will eat pieces of food that aren't edible in this realm. Sometimes, when a blood sacrifice is necessary, you can cut your hand and let it drip onto your altar, or any figures representing the gods.

But on an even more essential level, Gyfu instructs us to create reciprocal relationships with the people in our communities. I know that sometimes gift-giving can feel like a competition. There are certainly kindreds and other smaller heathen communities that experience this tit-for-tat gift-giving—and in these cases the gifting becomes toxic. That is not the kind of gifting that this rune instructs.

Norse society used gift-giving as a form of respect. Before the Viking age, wealth was not meant to be amassed—it was meant to be shared. Even in the family sagas, one of the markers of an enemy was someone who amassed gold for themselves, stealing from others and disrespecting their right to their own wealth and abundance.

From the perspective of a leftist heathen, the wealthy 1 percent hoarding their treasures while members of the community suffer is immoral. If you have enough for yourself, you need to give to the community. And if you are living with poverty, you are encouraged to ask for assistance.

It is also essential to ask for help—from your community, from the ancestors, from your gods—and Heathenry makes room for the asking specifically. There is a sense that what goes around comes around—that if you are in need of help now, you will be able to help others later. Growing up in a farming community, you still see this to this day. My parents live really rural, and they have whole networks of people who can help with specific things. They have found people to help them with fixing things around the house, auto mechanics, driveway repair, seeding the fields—the list goes on and on. This gifting is still essential in all communities. One of the things that I missed the most during the pandemic years is communal experiences, like potlucks and helping people move or have a garage sale. I vividly remember reading a book and in the story there was a barn raising. All of the people in the village got together to work on this project, with people cooking in the kitchen to keep everyone fed. Now, I can't lie to you and say that I have participated in many agricultural group projects, but this sense of a community coming together to work toward a shared goal is something that I miss in my bones.

Of course, the pandemic and uprisings have highlighted the need for increased networks for mutual aid. Networks popped up across the Twin Cities. Some of them were temporary, some of them are still going at the time of writing this book. They don't need to be permanent for their impact to be felt. These networks are a beautiful example of solidarity in action, of the true spirit of creating reciprocal communities in order to create safe communities.

Gyfu is not just a gift, but an oath: that you will use what has been given for the greater good.

Rune	Transliteration	International Phonetic Alphabet	Proto-Germanic Name	Meaning
X̱	g	/g/	Gebo, gyfu	gift

ANGLO-SAXON RUNE POEM:

Generosity brings credit and honour, which support one's dignity;
it furnishes help and subsistence
to all broken men who are devoid of aught else.

Opportunities for Ancestral Discovery

Read the *Hávamál*, and in particular the stanzas about gift-giving (especially stanzas 1–4, 39–49). What resonates with you? What feels a little off?

Think about the kinds of things that your ancestors would have created and given away as gifts. These can be baked goods, milk, cheese, chopped wood, clothing—anything that might have been traded or gifted. What are some objects that you were given by family that have a history? How can you repay this gift, or pay it forward?

RADICAL GYFU

- What things count as gifts? Are there any qualifiers to what a gift is to you? Do you have any ideas left over from capitalism that people need to "earn" gifts?

- When was the last time you gave a gift? When was the last time you received a gift?

- What does the term mutual aid mean to you?

- How do you engage in acts of mutual aid? How can you make a commitment to do more mutual aid moving forward?

WUNJO

Keywords: joy, happiness, contentment, thriving

Wunjo is one of the absolute sweetest runes in the entire Futhark and shows the range of expression in this oracle. It contains all of the optimism of our journey with the runes so far, and a promise of more to come. Wunjo is also a deceptively simple rune, but there are a great many lessons embedded here. There is little point to things without joy.

I know so many people who come to tarot or divination for the purpose of laying bare their pain, of dealing explicitly with difficult and even traumatic situations. Or sometimes, we turn to divination to help us find a new direction. We may feel aimless, or we may have too many ideas and not be sure what to prioritize or even what steps to take. Typically people don't seek answers if they are fully content with their lives. And yet, how do we know when it's okay to stop striving? How do we know when we've reached happiness?

What is the shape of joy?

Whenever I write or speak about Wunjo, it takes me a while to formulate my thoughts. Because the meaning of this rune is fairly simple—joy, happiness—there isn't actually that much written about it in the lore. Often other rune books feel . . . not quite lacking, not hollow, but they feel incomplete when it comes to Wunjo. There aren't wildly divergent ideas about the rune, not as much chatter about "does it mean this or that." Is it really this easy? Is it possible that it's this beautiful?

We are accustomed to building stories around struggle. Think of your favorite novel, or movie, or any kind of story. The plot revolves around some kind of conflict. Romance is the one genre that I can think of where the main characters are led by joy. Yes, there's always some kind of conflict (oh no, they're dating someone else, miscommunications leading to temporary breakups, and the like), but romance always ends with a happily-ever-after or a happy-for-now. And romance is also one of the genres that is scoffed at for being too "fluffy" or too feminine.

Joy is personal. Yes, it is an emotion that is contagious—you can share it with others—but ultimately we all have our own definition of what joy looks like. A lot of people (myself included) often think of happiness like "I'll know it when I see it." But what does happiness feel like?

We can plan our creative projects, our careers, our relationships, always striving for that feeling. Society prescribes certain life tracks. These are often culturally determined. I know that growing up, I felt like all around me there were examples of people who had careers, staying in the same job for decades, with a loving spouse, children, owning a home, going on tropical vacations . . . the whole kit. There's a whole lot of privilege in the assumption that this is an ideal life.

I think about that life, and I feel suffocated. There are some aspects of it that I can easily see myself loving—particularly a loving spouse, and going on vacations. But having one job for decades? I can't stomach that. I don't care if that makes other people happy, but I want to stay far away from that lifestyle personally. And I know many people who can't fathom wanting children, but I also know other people who yearn for children and don't feel complete without them.

Joy isn't replicable; it's not an equation. There's no set of factors that if you plug them in, your result is happiness.

We all know it doesn't work that way. We may be taught this is how we're "supposed" to operate—that life is one progression from milestone to milestone—but the truth is that it's much more twisty-turny than that. Sequestering yourself into a vision of what "should" make you happy is a pretty surefire way to feel terrible.

The last few years of my life have been about reclaiming my own joy. Whether that joy was stolen from me by my abusers, the oppressive overculture, or even my own ideas of what "should" make me happy, I've been getting curious about what actually makes me happy.

But here's the thing: we have a really hard time noticing when things are good.

I've seen people talk about this online as a survival instinct. Humans are trained to notice patterns and to notice when things are off because our brains are still in survival mode. It's that kind of pseudoscience that people talk about at cocktail parties. No one is able to cite the source; there's just this feeling. But I would challenge everyone reading this to try to consciously notice when things are good. I would argue that this too is a necessary survival instinct.

This is also Wunjo: accepting ourselves as an ecstatic part of nature, accepting ourselves as who we are. My desires are just as valid as anyone else's. That shouldn't be a radical idea, and yet somehow it is. So here are some things that bring me joy. Taking myself out for a nice coffee and reading silly fiction might seem unnecessary to a capitalist cog in the machine, but I've learned that these things *are* important. It's these things that nourish the self I've buried deep under societal expectations and norms.

Joy is a radical feeling for queer people and people of color.

In a society that has long profited on our trauma and our pain, a society that benefits from us keeping our heads down and not making waves, our joy is a sacred rebellion.[33] Queer people are also known for creating new systems, new ways of experiencing joy. It's not just about what we have, but it's also about what we build. Part of the system of capitalism is the false idea that you are always wanting, that there is always more you should be buying. It's a system built around the myth of lack, that you lack the goods necessary to be happy. "Buy this thing—unlock happiness" is a classic marketing ploy, if not the only marketing ploy.

Finding innate happiness, without the stuff, is an act of rebellion.

And if you are a woman, trans, queer, a person of color? Your smile has them shaking in their boots.

When Wunjo comes up, let yourself indulge. Set yourself up for happiness—whatever that looks like for you. Find time every day to

---

33   brown, *Pleasure Activism.*

indulge in something that is purely joyful, and purely for you. I find this also means that you may need some space—find blank spots in your schedule and indulge in something. Buy yourself that decadent chocolate truffle. Bathe in a sunny spot with your cat. Go for a walk around your neighborhood. Read your favorite book from childhood.

Wunjo is here because you are enough, we are enough, and you need to celebrate yourself.

Rune	Transliteration	International Phonetic Alphabet	Proto-Germanic Name	Meaning
ᚹ	w	/w/	Wunjo	joy

ANGLO-SAXON RUNE POEM:

Bliss he enjoys who knows not suffering, sorrow nor anxiety,
and has prosperity and happiness and a good enough house.

Opportunities for Ancestral Discovery

The things that create happiness have changed culturally over the years. What folk tales can you think of that show happiness? What does "happily ever after" look like in these stories?

Think about the lives your ancestors must have led. What would be cause for celebration? Are there specific times of year, or perhaps holidays, that would have been especially important? And how can you adapt that to your everyday now?

RADICAL WUNJO

- When was the last time you felt joy? Where did you feel it in your body?

- Laughter helps us release muscle tension and triggers good endorphins. Get yourself into a good space, and pretend to laugh. Make yourself laugh until it becomes real laughter. Write about how that felt.

- Write out a list of all the things that make you happy. Return to this list when you're feeling depressed, and choose something to do and/or engage with.

- What does queer joy mean to you? Is it gender euphoria? Being with your lover? Being out in queer community? Write about your experience of queer joy.

5

The Second Ætt

HAGALAZ

Keywords: hail, storm, danger, shelter-in-place, disaster

This is the first rune of the second ætt in the Futhark. After the steady growth of the first ætt, this can feel like a pretty rude awakening. Hail? We start the second ætt with hail?

Hagalaz feels as though this is another sort of initiation: if you've been doing spiritual work for some time, you come to a point where it's no longer about feel-good wisdom to get you through the day. Our spiritual journeys force us to confront the darker aspects of ourselves, to wrestle with our trauma as well as our purpose. This isn't light stuff—and Hagalaz, the hail, is the wake-up call to this difficult spiritual work.

Hagalaz is the harbinger of dark change. It can feel a lot like both the Death card and the Tower card in tarot. The Tower is one of my favorite cards in the tarot. It represents the destruction of false foundations; it destroys what you know so that you can build something different and more in alignment with your values. Harnessing the energy of the Tower is incredibly important in leftist circles, particularly as we work to break down the foundations of white male supremacy, heteronormativity, and capitalism. For many (especially white) people, this process will be distinctly uncomfortable. We have to see our privilege, understand it, and consciously choose discomfort to create a different kind of world. Where the Tower is a wrecking ball, crashing in without ceremony to raze our bullshit to the ground, Hagalaz forces you to sit with it, to really see it, and gives you the opportunity to choose something different. Hagalaz forces us to confront our past—especially actions that we are not proud of. Norse mythic cycles are always hurtling toward destruction and regrowth.

Hagalaz is often associated with Hel, Norse goddess of the underworld. Her body is half alive and half dead. She represents the lurking presence of death in the Norse world. Odin may be the Allfather, but Death is the one that comes for all in the end. Hel as the "hidden"[1] shows she is in charge of the dead who are buried or cremated and whose souls are invisible to the living. Basically, Hel takes all of the things that have died outside of a noble death in battle and brings them to her realm. In fact, she is sometimes seen as a poetic personification of the underworld—and not fully a deity in her own right. She is primordial, outside of the realm of the Aesir. Somehow, Hel is simultaneously a place, a goddess, and a job.

The first written record of Hel comes from Snorri Sturluson in the 13th-century retelling of the Gylfaginning.[2] She is mentioned as one of Loki's three children, all of whom are fated to bring about the end of the world during Ragnarök. Like Loki, Hel is not a member of the Aesir or the Vanir. She is even more of an outsider than he is, because she is not adopted by any of the gods and is instead banished into her realms.

Now let's talk about some personal gnosis of mine surrounding Hel. Hel is not actually Loki's daughter—she is only Loki's daughter in so much as he reveals that which should not be revealed. She is deeply connected with the Norns. They are beings of fate, who are able to see

---

1   Kvilhaug, *The Seed of Yggdrasil.*
2   Sturluson, *The Prose Edda.*

the ripples and the ways that one life touches another. Of course, the way that we die is connected with our ørlog intimately. If we have Urðr (past precedence), Verðandi (present moment), and Skuld (what should happen), it only makes sense to me that Hel (hidden one) is in charge of the way we will die. She is also in a league of her own. I have often thought of her as a lone wolf—only she can do the job that she has been given, and she does it solitary. She seems to stand aside from the Aesir. Ymir's death and the dissolution of his body are what created the nine realms. The birth-death-rebirth cycle hinges on death as a transformation into our next incarnation.

Hel is a busy goddess, much like other Death deities were also very busy (Hades and Anubis come to mind). A lot of things die, and a lot of things need to be ushered into the next world. In the Gylfaginning[3] Sturluson claims that Hel is the ruler of the nine realms—that is a lot of responsibility. Kvilhaug writes in *The Seed of Yggdrasil* that it's possible that Hel is the ruler of these nine realms because they are mortal realms.[4] Death is the ultimate judgment of all mortal beings, and so she rules over these realms—not Odin, the wanderer, "Allfather." It is death that has the final guidance.

Hel is a great equalizer. For queer folks, she is the understanding that we are all subject to the same laws of physics, the same laws of mortality. Hel is also a great connector. Heathenry relies so intensely on ancestral veneration and connection with the wisdom of those who came before us that Hel becomes a connector. When we are working on connecting with our queer ancestors, Hel operates as a link in the chain.

When you journey to the gates of Hel's underworld, you need to ask to be seen. This is clear from the myth of the Death of Baldr. In the myth, Loki tricks Baldr's brother into shooting him with an arrow made of mistletoe, which is the only thing in the world that has not promised to harm him. When Baldr dies, he is taken by Hel. The gods grieve Baldr deeply—as God of Light, Poetry, Song, and so much beauty, he was sorely missed. Frigg asks if there is anyone who would volunteer to ride to Helheim to beg for Hel to release Baldr. Hermöðr volunteers, and though he makes

---

3   Sturluson, *The Prose Edda.*
4   Kvilhaug, *The Seed of Yggdrasil.*

it all the way to the gates of Helheim, he is met by Móðguðr, Hel's maid. Because Hermöðr is a living being he is not allowed to enter Helheim. Eventually he jumps the wall and finds himself in Hel's hall, where they are celebrating Baldr's life with many treasures and a feast. Hel agrees to release Baldr if every being in the world weeps for him. Of course, Loki disguises himself as a giantess and refuses to weep for Baldr so Hel refuses to release him.

This is ultimately an act of cruel grace. The fact that Baldr has died and is forbidden to return to the gods means that he is not able to fight during Ragnarök. In the end, Baldr is released from Helheim after the battle and he goes on to help recreate the world as one of beauty and love. It is Hel's judgment and boundaries that allow for this to occur. Baldr is the most potent symbol of resurrection in Norse myth, but it is only through Hel that he is able to transform and return to rebuild the world. First comes the underworld journey, then comes the daybreak.

Queer Hagalaz is hail breaking through expectations and propriety. Queer Hagalaz is different gender identities shining off of a big hailstone—a hailstone that is a giant fuck you to compulsory heterosexuality. Hagalaz is not just a weapon for us to use, however. When turned against queer folks it is your parents disowning you because of your sexuality and/or gender. When turned against queer people Hagalaz is laws passed restricting gender-affirming health care in places you didn't think that would ever happen. Hagalaz is shock and devastation. We can only hope we are the ones to wield it, and it is not wielded against us.

It took me a long time to understand why the rune poems referred to Hagalaz as the hail-seed. I associate hail with destruction, and that is how a lot of modern practitioners see hail. Here in the upper Midwest, we occasionally have devastating hailstorms. Hail can ruin crops, fields, and roofs, and break all the windows in your car. It is a force of nature and difficult to predict. Kari Tauring talks about how Hel takes death and creates the next level of life. Sometimes, you need to burn it to the ground and start over. That is the seed of Hagalaz: the seed of destruction to create something different.

Rune	Transliteration	International Phonetic Alphabet	Proto-Germanic Name	Meaning
ᚺ ᚻ	h	/h/	Hagalaz	hail

ANGLO-SAXON RUNE POEM:

Hail is the whitest of grain;
it is whirled from the vault of heaven
and is tossed about by gusts of wind
and then it melts into water.

ICELANDIC RUNE POEM:

Hail
cold grain
and shower of sleet
and sickness of serpents.

NORWEGIAN RUNE POEM:

Hail is the coldest of grain;
Christ created the world of old.

Opportunities for Ancestral Discovery

Take some time to research the concepts of the underworld, in both Norse cosmology and other myth cycles. What have you learned? What resonates with you?

Create a map of the underworld, as you imagine it. Where do your ancestors reside? Where do the Mighty Dead reside?

RADICAL HAGALAZ

- Change is essential for anyone working for liberation. What changes are you seeking? How can you use the destructive force of Hagalaz to make that change happen?

- Hagalaz, hail-seed. What seeds are you planting, though they may not come to fruition for a long time?

- What needs to be cleared from your life, on a personal level? What do you need to make room for, and what can go?

NAUTHIZ

Keywords: need, needfire, Norns, imbalance

Nauthiz comes after Hagalaz. Needs become clear when what we know has been razed to the ground, trampled, fallen. There is an urgency to Nauthiz that can be destabilizing. It is truly a fire born of friction, tension between things that need to come to a head. The rune itself even resembles two twigs or flint stones rubbing together—friction creates the fire.

This is a rune of fire, but not in the way that a lot of people think about fire in magic. Yes, it is a rune of power—but all runes contain power. As with all runes, the different rune poems show different meanings and layers to these runes. In the Icelandic rune poem, the rune suggests a relationship between need and oppression.[5] This is a beacon of light, but specifically a call to those who experience marginalization— to see the full extent of the oppression and to find a way out.

When you place these runes in progression, you must recognize the folly of your past in order to see the potential futures available to you. This helps to contextualize the present and further define the futures that we actually want. Sometimes, Nauthiz shows up as a roadblock. If you are continuously running into walls, you need to examine if the challenge is trying to teach you something. The setback is a teacher, or a guide. It's a sign that you need to rethink what you're doing—because success might do more harm to the community around you than good. Nauthiz can show up to help us reprioritize our needs over our wants. In this way Nauthiz has power in the most basic aspects of our lives: where we live, what we eat, our relationships. It is shelter, nutrition, love when we need it the most. Nauthiz is the bare bones. Nauthiz is the baseline, the starting position.

---

5   "Rune Poems," Wikisource.

Kari Tauring talks about Nauthiz as Gyfu out of balance.[6] When you look at the runes next to each other, you can see that Gyfu is a full "X," but Nauthiz has one leg shorter than the other. Need happens when someone in the community is taking more than their fair share and not giving back. This rune points toward deep inequality and injustice at the same time that it can help us figure out the solution. This rune asks us to figure out what justice looks like to us, in our situations of pain. It asks us to envision a future where we have what we need and are able to recover from catastrophe without falling even further into debt.

In a reading, this rune points toward what is needed. For example, if you are asking about how to handle a tricky work situation, any rune that you read after Nauthiz (whether thrown on the cloth or drawn from a cup) is a literal action step or resource that is necessary to resolution. In a reading about health, Nauthiz instructs us on how to best take care of ourselves in the healing process.

Nauthiz is also helpful in swift communication with the gods. Bonfires are used as traditional prayer methods. You build a fire, and when it is huge and lighting your full circle, you send your prayers to the gods. Anything that you need the gods to hear, say it into the flames of the bonfire and it will carry your prayers to their ears. But the form of sacred fire that Nauthiz is most closely related to is a needfire. This is a fire ritual from across Northern Europe—including Scandinavia.

It has actually been documented by folklorists who were preserving information at the turn of the last century. I think it's kind of funny to look at how folklorists describe the ritual, and then how I know it. There are some interesting differences, though the folklorists did record the gist of it. According to the 1911 *Encyclopedia Brittanica,*[7] the needfire is a community ritual to ward off disease from their herds and flocks. The farmers would get together to create a fire through the oldest known means: friction from rubbing two sticks together, or a flint stone. In this version of the *Encyclopedia Brittanica,* needfire rites are recorded from Scotland, the Hebrides, Germany, and Scandinavia. In trolldom all fires in the village would be put out and a torch would

6   Tauring, *The Runes.*
7   "Need-Fire," 1911 *Encyclopædia Britannica.*

be carried from home to home, lighting the central hearth. This was spreading the blessings and protection of the needfire.[8]

So, we're modern heathens: why are we reading from a 1911 *Encyclopedia Brittanica*? There were a lot of problems with that era of folkloric recording, but it's also important to return to these texts. Europeans were particularly interested in this romantic vision of Europe, and many used that romanticism to assert that European cultures were superior to other cultures, as I described in chapter 3.

In general, there is a lot to be said in criticism of early folklore and anthropology studies and how those were collected. However, as many of these folkloric practices died out by the middle of the 20th century, these biased accounts are essential records for understanding folkloric practices. These accounts must be read carefully, balanced with contemporary research and a good understanding of the historic circumstances during which they were recorded. Another good source for folklore is actually accounts of "rational" people who were ridiculing the old ways. Without realizing it, many of these accounts preserved the folklore for centuries.

The needfire is not one of those rituals that has totally died. It has a legacy of practice beyond the 1800s and is still practiced today. This is a powerful rite that you can adapt to your contemporary folk magic practice and use to bolster your own kindred, chosen family, and queer community. Build a needfire and invite all of your friends over. Instruct them to bring their own candles. Slowly, have everyone go around and say what they need protection from and blessings for the most. Once they have spoken their needs aloud, instruct them to light their candles from the needfire.

There are so many needs that are specific to the queer community—so many needs to be uplifted by the powerful blessing of the needfire. The need to be seen and loved for who you truly are—in spite of cis-hetero-normativity. The need for gender-affirming health care, to have access to hormone replacement therapy, top surgery, and reproductive care. The need to live in a place where housing and employment

---

8   Gårdbäck, *Trolldom*.

won't be put at risk by coming out of the closet. The need to have full autonomy over our bodies. The need to live without the threat of terror attacks and violence.

The ritual of the needfire also reminds us that this protection and blessing is active. Yes, it is divine, but the spell is cast by all of us. The needfire helps us to reach out to the divine in the most difficult times, as well as support one another in community.

One really interesting thing about the concept of fate in Norse mythology is that it isn't sealed. While Skuld is undoubtedly tied to the future, there is a sense of individual determination. The Norns are conceived of as constantly weaving their web, changing things in response to the choices that people make. I see the Norns creating a sort of choose-your-own-adventure: they present the right questions at the right time. Odin would not spend so much time trying to fight off Ragnarök if that weren't possible. Yes, fate exists in this cosmology, but not in a static way.

Skuld asks you what steps you need to take to have the best possible outcome. You are invited into a visionary practice, imagining new and beautiful futures that you can help build. And those wishes get woven into Wunjo and other runes.

Build your own needfire, and evaluate where you are most needed in this world.

Rune	Transliteration	International Phonetic Alphabet	Proto-Germanic Name	Meaning
ᚾ	n	/n/	Nauthiz	need

ANGLO-SAXON RUNE POEM:

Trouble is oppressive to the heart;
yet often it proves a source of help and salvation
to the children of men, to everyone who heeds it betimes.

ICELANDIC RUNE POEM:

> *Constraint*
> *grief of the bond-maid*
> *and state of oppression*
> *and toilsome work.*

NORWEGIAN RUNE POEM:

> *Constraint gives scant choice;*
> *a naked man is chilled by the frost.*

Opportunities for Ancestral Discovery

It's important when doing ancestor work to think about what people may have lacked. What would our ancestors have desperately wanted, but not had access to? How can we work with and relate to that? How can you honor them now, and honor the hardships they went through?

You are your ancestors' wildest dreams. They want you to do well, to feel good. Think of getting your needs met—all of them, including laughter and love—and ask the ancestors what steps you need to take. Journal their answers here.

RADICAL NAUTHIZ

- What is a need? The crux of this rune is to help us distinguish between our needs and our wants. In order for you to be happy, what do you absolutely need?

- In what ways do you put off getting your own needs met?

- It's time to get visionary. What needs are not being met in your society right now?

- Which of your own needs are not being met?

- What are some ways that you can begin to meet your own needs, while also working to make sure that more people are getting their own needs met?

ISA

Keywords: ice, stillness, frozen, boundary

Isa represents ice: that which is frozen. It is a barrier. It is water that has become so still, it has been made solid. Ice is one of the elements that signaled the birth of our world.

To my Scandinavian ancestors, ice was a harbinger of difficult times. While life didn't necessarily stop in the winter months, many things were more difficult. This represented a pause in the growth cycle, a time to hunker down with your family and kindred to withstand the long dark of Scandinavian winter. In the rune poems, ice looms and is represented as an element of hardship. When Isa is present, movement is difficult and it's hard to trust yourself and your environment.

The creation of the world in Norse cosmology happens in two underworlds: Niflheim and Muspelheim.

The bridge between Muspelheim and Niflheim is how we can access the courage to make change happen. These are also the two realms that centered in the Norse creation myth. In the beginning, before chaos, there was a formless void. Then, the icy rivers of Niflheim met the dazzling flames of Muspelheim, and from this joining the giant Ymir was born, thus creating chaos. When Ymir was slain, from his body the world was created. It is the combination of fire and ice in Norse thought that created the world.

Isa, ice, is associated with the Norn Verðandi, the present. But the present is inextricably linked to the past. Without the past, the present doesn't exist. I see Urðr and Verðandi holding hands, each working together to help us get focused in the present. You have to be incredibly present when you're walking on ice—one wrong movement and you could topple over. You need to listen carefully as you cross the ice on a lake, because the ice will tell you if you're about to go under.

Ice is a very intimidating element, and one that you may misunderstand if you don't live in a place that gets intense winter. So often, we think of this rune as a standstill. But with Isa there is a choice: will you take stillness for rest, or will you be immobilized?

So now, if you have seen your life go up in flames, know that the ice is here to bring a chill, to help you pause long enough to set order. Isa can represent a sacred pause, a time to gather ourselves and gather our strength. It is deep rest. It is making sure that we are protected. Hagalaz is the storm that breaks down the tower. Nauthiz is the action you take to get your needs met in the aftermath. And Isa is the chill that allows you to bring clear thinking to your next steps.

That is the medicine to be found here. If you have a longstanding meditation practice or know someone with a meditation practice, you've probably encountered the movement within stillness. It may not feel like you're doing much, but the cumulative effect is beautiful. From times of deep stillness, you will find the ability to think clearly and calmly about your next steps. Sometimes you might feel anxious about not knowing your next steps, but it's important to sit with these difficult feelings. Until you feel them, you will always run from them.

It's no secret that the ice of the world is diminishing. Global climate change has melted glaciers; whole shelves of ice have separated and melted in Antarctica. We are living in a time when we actually want more ice—it is the loss of these resources that signals danger for us now. I would be remiss in this section if I didn't talk about the dangers of climate change—and working with Isa magically to assist our actions against the warming planet.

As the glacial ice melts, the warming of the planet accelerates. I have personally worked with Isa to help calm myself and deal with the heat better on extra-hot days. I've also worked with Isa when praying for a milder climate in the summertime, just picturing the rune as an icicle and offering up my voice and desire for a more livable planet. I will say that the best climate magic is always paired with action. Plant a garden, donate to environmental justice organizations, and volunteer with climate justice organizations in your area.

For the queer practitioner Isa has another added layer: powerful self-protection and disguise.

I wouldn't go so far as to say that Isa signifies staying in the closet, but it can represent the fear of coming out only to be frozen or iced out of your family. You might be afraid of being pulled under, falling through the ice to be trapped if you don't come out. It all depends on the reading and other runes that show up surrounding Isa. Ice can be deceiving—and that is a quality that you can use for your own protection as a queer person.

Isa helps us to understand the ways that we hide ourselves. It can also allow us to take an extra moment away from the heat of a situation and find time for introspection. Another function of ice is a natural mirror—sometimes you can see yourself in the reflection of the ice. Do you appreciate what you see? Do you wish for something different? Sometimes when we hold a mirror up to a situation we find ourselves thinking about how we can clearly shift and change that situation. It reflects back all the ugly things that we wish we had done differently or ways of being we want to live up to. Allow Isa to provide that period of grace and reflection for you.

Isa can also offer protection within challenging situations. It allows you to find that beautiful place of stillness and stick to your own convictions. The ice can also deter people who would want to disrupt our queer communities, slow down police breaking up a protest, and generally speaking create an added layer of protection.

Rune	Transliteration	International Phonetic Alphabet	Proto-Germanic Name	Meaning
Ι	i	/i(:)/	Isa	ice

ANGLO-SAXON RUNE POEM:

Ice is very cold and immeasurably slippery;
it glistens as clear as glass and most like to gems;
it is a floor wrought by the frost, fair to look upon.

ICELANDIC RUNE POEM:

> *Ice*
> *bark of rivers*
> *and roof of the wave*
> *and destruction of the doomed.*

NORWEGIAN RUNE POEM:

> *Ice we call the broad bridge;*
> *the blind man must be led.*

Opportunities for Ancestral Discovery

Think about ice, and how your ancestors would have used it. Was the coming of the ice welcome?

Ice is used for preservation. Even to this day, we use ice to preserve our food. But so much else is preserved in the ice. Scientists use glacier ice cores to track big changes on the earth over time. What has the ice preserved of your ancestors?

RADICAL ISA

- What does ice mean to you? How do you interact with ice on a daily basis?

- What do you want to see preserved? What in your present situation needs to be captured and carried forward?

- Spend a full week meditating every day. Write down any insights you've gained, any surprises, or just any shifts in mindset.

JERA

Keywords: year, harvest, abundance, cycles of life

Jera is the reward for doing the hard work necessary to thrive. Jera represents abundance, the year and passage of time, and also harvest festivals. The Anglo-Saxon rune poem refers to Jera as summer, as joyful, a time of light and happiness. You can think of this rune as the energetic personification of the warm half of the year, as well as all of the work that needed to happen during this time. But this rune is also associated with the harvest, as in the reward for all of the hard work.

This rune is in the exact middle of the Futhark, and so I tend to think of it as an indicator of the summer solstice or winter solstice. I see this rune coming up in Midsommar because it's not just about harvest: it's about the work that we put into our efforts. Midsommar is a time when you're working with all aspects of the growing season. There are some things that are ready to be harvested (at least, here in Minnesota that's when we're harvesting blueberries and some early vegetables), but farmers are also planting, and tending to crops that are already planted.

At the same time, Jul comes right after a big harvest time. We do most of our harvests in the fall. In *Runes: A Deeper Journey*, Kari Tauring talks about how there are three different harvests in the Norse world: Grain Harvest, Fruit Harvest, and Meat Harvest. These harvests come at different times, and there was an assumption that if someone had a very good harvest, but their neighbor suffered a year of blight, that the bounty would be shared. So here again we see this idea of mutual aid and looking out for other members of the community.

There is a constancy to Jera because of the way it represents a full year—it is not the new year, it is the full year. This means it also represents the full spectrum of the growing season, including the time when the earth is resting in winter. Even the shape of this rune is cyclical—when you look at it, Jera seems to have a sort of momentum and forward movement. It always looks like one spoke is ready to turn over into another. Perhaps the "points" of the spokes are Midsommar and Jul, but they are just the major points on which the year turns.

Jera is not just about the year; it is also related to earth itself. This is a rune of appreciation of the gifts of nature, as well as of cultivation. The shape of the rune—two v's turned on their side and intertwining—speaks to me of cycles. This has always spoken to me of the cycles and seasons that recur year after year, the patterns within a set of bounded time. The shape is strangely reminiscent of the astrological symbol for Cancer, with a mirror image turning on itself. And just like the sign of Cancer, Jera has a nurturing energy.

Jera is a rune of ecological harmony. It is the joy of rebirth, that same joy that comes every springtime. Jera asks us how we can be in better harmony with the land. Yes, this is a harvest rune, but practitioners agree that it is a rune of slow growth. This is the kind of growth and harvest that comes from working with natural cycles, rather than against them. We have such an intense attitude of progress, of making things happen faster and faster, that to slow down and actually align yourself with nature is a radical act in itself. Jera invites you into this ecology, invites you to recognize that you are but a small part of the whole, and that you need to work with natural cycles rather than against them.

Jera is a rune of fecundity.

I associate this rune with Freyr, Freyja, and the Vanir. Freyr and Freyja are not Aesir, they are Vanir—which is a different tribe of gods. As the *Völuspá* tells it, the war between the Vanir and the Aesir was settled after both sides agreed to send people to basically live with the other side. Not exactly a hostage situation, but more like a peace offering in the form of people, like the kind of peace that was bought by intermarriage of royalty. It is in this way that Freyr, Freyja, and Njörðr are the three of the Vanir that come to live among the Aesir.

In speaking with a lot of different heathens, they have described the Vanir as being closer to nature deities. They are more about receiving good graces from the land, perhaps closer to the elves and other spirits. I like to think of the Vanir as being closer to the "feeling" self. The Aesir tend to be more closely related to human matters and the "thinking" brain. I spoke briefly about Njörðr on my podcast—he is the god of the sea, but specifically our relationship with the sea. Freyr and Freyja are also deities associated with nature—though I would say Freyr is even more associated with nature than Freyja is.

I have used this rune magically in my garden for a couple of years now. I originally got the idea for this ritual from Diana Paxson's *Taking Up the Runes*,[9] but I have changed it to better suit my own relationship with the rune. At the beginning of the growing season as you are planting your garden, trace the outline of Jera into the dirt. Say whatever hopes and dreams you have for the garden that year over the rune. Chant the name Jera several times, and feel yourself activating the rune's energy in the soil. If you would like to add more here, I also like to recite the Nine Herbs Charm, which is a Saxon charm for healing and protection.

Looking at specifically queer associations with harvest, I see this as a moment of being celebrated by and among your chosen family and friends for being exactly who you are. There is a sense of celebration in this rune and homecoming. It is also noteworthy that the summer solstice comes during the month of Pride—a celebration of the fullness of queer life and how far we've come. This is a time to be active, to be seen in community and come together.

Rune	Transliteration	International Phonetic Alphabet	Proto-Germanic Name	Meaning
ᛃ	j	/j/	Jera	year, good year, harvest

ANGLO-SAXON RUNE POEM:

Summer is a joy to men, when God, the holy King of Heaven,
suffers the earth to bring forth shining fruits
for rich and poor alike.

---

9 Paxson, *Taking Up the Runes.*

ICELANDIC RUNE POEM:

> *Plenty*
> *boon to men*
> *and good summer*
> *and thriving crops.*

NORWEGIAN RUNE POEM:

> *Plenty is a boon to men;*
> *I say that Frothi was generous.*

Opportunities for Ancestral Discovery

What did the growing season look like where your ancestors were from?

Research harvest festivals from wherever your ancestors hail. What do you notice? Are there ways that you can pay tribute to your ancestors on specific harvest festivals now?

RADICAL JERA

- In what ways do you connect with nature? How can you connect more with nature?

- Think about your year. The old harvest festivals and the Wheel of the Year don't always make sense, given where you may be living now. Think about the natural shifts that happen in your year. Write out your own "wheel."

- Reading suggestion: *Braiding Sweetgrass* by Robin Wall Kimmerer. This book has big Jera energy.

- Make a list of all the plants that you engage with the most. This could also be essential oils that you love the smell of, or spices that you always reach for in the kitchen. Now, look up some of their properties. Are there any themes? Do you have a strong balance? What other plants would bring this more into balance?

EIWAZ

Keywords: yew tree, death, transition, movement between the worlds, underworld, hunting/conflict

Eiwaz, yew tree, rune of sacred transition. This is the first of the "tree" runes in the Elder Futhark. Yews are ancient—there are living yew trees that are five hundred to one thousand years old. They have seen things that we can't imagine. They are an invitation to explore, a question, eldritch trees in the best sense. Like the yew, Eiwaz is an invitation. This is the perfect rune to use in trance work to meet the nine realms. It has roots deep into the underworld and branches high into the heavens. The trunk is like a backbone, keeping things stable for the nine realms. This rune can also act as a stabilizing force for us. Use it to ground your work and help push you into new heights.

Many heathens think of Yggdrasil as a yew, or as an ash. Yggdrasil contains the realms of death and the heavens; it is the Axis Mundi of Norse cosmology, acting as a bridge between all of the realms. Any tree can be an avatar of Yggdrasil, and there are compelling reasons in the source works for many different trees. Perhaps Yggdrasil changes species based on the person viewing it, or the reason you are going on a journey to seek Yggdrasil. Perhaps the tree is itself a shapeshifter, as difficult to pin down as Loki.

The yew is a fascinating tree, both biologically and in folklore. Yew is an evergreen tree, which typically have associations with rebirth and standing up to adversity. The yew is a little more complicated, as it is one of the evergreen trees that is also associated with death. All parts of the yew tree are poisonous except for the flesh of the berry. Poisonous plants have a special place in witchcraft—they are key ingredients in flying ointments, creating the perfect biological reaction to send you on a wild trip.

And yet there are many paradoxes with this tree—the poison of the tree comes from alkaloids known as taxines, and yet it also produces taxanes that are used in medicine to fight cancer—particularly breast and lung cancer. Taxol is the most well-known naturally derived cancer drug and makes up an important part of chemotherapy. According to the National Cancer Institute, taxol is used to treat cervical cancer, endometrial cancer, lung cancer, ovarian cancer, thymic carcinoma, and carcinoma of an unknown primary.[10] The taxanes used to produce Taxol come from the bark of the Pacific yew. It is a very harsh medicine—but an essential one.

Magically, you could say that the yew tree is the imperative that in order to heal, you need to be able to hex. In this way the yew represents the full spectrum of life. It is able to move us through the different stages of life and death and rebirth all in one. This is essential for the world tree, because it must contain all of lived experience within its branches and roots. Eiwaz is therefore connected to transformation on a deep level.

Another important thing to note about the yew tree is that they have a gender binary of their own—there are "male" trees (the ones that release pollen) and "female" trees (the ones that produce berries). There are other species of tree that contain all of the sexual characteristics in a single individual, but the yew is not one of them. That's particularly interesting because for the longest time I associated my gender fluidity with the yew tree because of its association with transformation, but now I see the yew as a particular ally for binary trans individuals. While writing this section, I was reading as much information about yew trees as I could find and I learned something incredible: one of the oldest living yew trees is changing its sex.[11] So while the yew is binary, it can transition—as do many other conifer tree species with binary sexes.

Because of the toxicity of the tree, the yew is often associated with cults of the dead. There are tales that when kings were sacrificed, they were poisoned with yew. Throughout the British Isles, churchyards were built around ancient yew trees. When I was in England I

---

10   "Success Story: Taxol," National Cancer Institute.
11   Izade, "One of Europe's Oldest Trees."

learned some folklore from a local. He said that churches were built around yew trees because pre-Christian people were already worshipping at the yew, so they placed the church there to lure more members of the congregation. It also makes sense to me that the early Christian missionaries would hear about the stories of death and rebirth on the yew, and decide that was an auspicious place for a church. Christianity is, after all, a death cult.

Beneath these legends is the archetype of the yew as threshold. The yew represents the connection of life and death, as well as all the liminal space between. Verðandi, Norn of Becoming, lives in that hair's breadth between life and death. It is a hedge-riding tree. It is a tree that facilitates spirit journeying and communication with the dead. Odin also uses Sleipnir to ride between different parts of the world tree. The eight-legged horse is ridden between the worlds, between branches and roots of the tree. Eiwaz and Ehwaz get connected in these moments, two runes coming together and then diverging. I'll be covering Ehwaz in the next season of the podcast, but for those of you who aren't familiar: Ehwaz is the horse, the steed, the ride.

Maria Kvilhaug writes in *The Seed of Yggdrasill* that you could conceive of the physical universe as a steed, or traveling vehicle, of what Odin really represents: Spirit. In this way we are all similar to Odin, as we are all spirits riding the world; our bodies are our steed. It is through this riding that we are able to experience the world—and that is another way that we are in partnership with Yggdrasil.[12]

To gain knowledge of the runes, Odin sacrificed himself to himself and hung for nine days and nine nights upon a tree. Not only is this a tale of death and rebirth, but it also shows the tree as a threshold to wisdom. Much like the Hanged Man in tarot, Eiwaz gives us a sense of suspension. Like Jera, it takes time to learn the mysteries. But there is something cosmic here, something beautiful. Odin is deeply associated with Yggdrasil for other reasons as well. In his role as the Hanged God, he hung from Yggdrasil's branches and journeyed through the spirit realm to find the runes. But we must not forget that Odin is also a god of

12   Kvilhaug, *The Seed of Yggdrasill.*

war.[13] He wandered the nine realms to gain wisdom, yes, but one of his primary goals in the myths is to learn as much as he can to prepare for Ragnarök. One of the faces of Yggdrasil is as a yew tree—and that has its own warlike associations.

The yew tree itself has long had associations with battle. Longbows were made out of yew wood, because it is extremely strong but also flexible. In *Grímnismál*, Odin tells us that the god Ullr is located in Ýdalir, a grove of yews.[14] Ullr is a god of the bow and snowshoes that we don't hear too much of in the myths. Longbows made new and different kinds of war possible for ancient peoples, covering so much more ground than they would have been able to cover previously with shortbows.[15] There is a sense of urgency building in this rune—when we think of a new weapon that can have great capacity to change the world, it does not usually bode well. This would have been a useful rune for Odin to have an understanding of as he was preparing for Ragnarök. The longbow wasn't used only in war—it was also used for successful hunting. When Eiwaz comes up alongside Algiz in particular, there is a sense that "the hunt is on"—and depending on the situation, you could be the hunter or the hunted.

A feeling of being hunted might be a problem for you when you are going through a particularly difficult shadow period. There are times in our lives when we are actually locked in battle with an adversary, a toxic friend, a coworker, or Goddess forbid, a stalker. This could also signify a feeling of being watched or judged—which to me, at least, often feels like being hunted. When you are feeling this, Eiwaz is here not only as a warning but also as a source of protection. An old Germanic adage translates to: "Before the yews, no harmful magic can remain." In the Balkans yew is still used as a protective amulet to keep away evil spirits. You can carry simple yew twigs or make them into a cross or upside-down triangle.[16]

The positive side of Eiwaz as a hunting rune comes from the lessons we learn as hunters ourselves. The "thing" I'm talking about here can be

13 Oates, *The Hanged God*.
14 Orchard, *Dictionary of Norse Myth*.
15 Tauring, *The Runes*.
16 Boyer, *Under the Witching Tree*.

literal subsistence hunting—but it can also be a metaphorical hunt, as in the hunt for a new home, the hunt for a particularly treasured kind of clothing or unique collector's item, and the hunt for knowledge or wisdom. That is a particularly Odinic interpretation of these two runes showing up together—the sly one always seeking wisdom and knowledge, and stopping at nothing to get it. I also think this could signify that you are searching for your spiritual path moving forward.

Eiwaz is therefore a good rune to work with for setting goals that are clear and manageable. It will help you plant firm roots that will allow you to move forward in a very good way.

Rune	Transliteration	International Phonetic Alphabet	Proto-Germanic Name	Meaning
ᛇ	ï (æ)	/æ:/	Eiwaz	yew tree

ANGLO-SAXON RUNE POEM:

The yew is a tree with rough bark,
hard and fast in the earth, supported by its roots,
a guardian of flame and a joy upon an estate.

ICELANDIC RUNE POEM:

Yew
bent bow
and brittle iron
and giant of the arrow.

NORWEGIAN RUNE POEM:

Yew is the greenest of trees in winter;
it is wont to crackle when it burns.

Opportunities for Ancestral Discovery

What are some death customs in your family? What did death transitions look like for your ancestors?

Research the different realms of the dead as found on Yggdrasil. There are many different ways that the dead were sheperded into the afterlife. What realm of the dead makes the most sense to you? Where would you like to go?

RADICAL EIWAZ

- Meditate on Eiwaz. Practice a meditation through all nine realms of Yggdrasil, riding the yew tree from realm to realm. Write out a reflection.

- As queer people, we have a specific kind of relationship with death. Many of our queer ancestors were taken from us too young. Think about the queer ancestors, those who have inspired you in your own understanding of self. Journal about your reflections here.

- Take nine nights to meditate at midnight. Bring your rune set with you, but don't do anything with it. On the ninth night, cast your runes. Write everything that comes to mind, stream-of-conscious style.

PERTH/PERTHRO

Keywords: mystery, luck, unknown

Perth is the great unknowing. This is one of the most frustrating runes, because there isn't a clear etymological root for it. It was substituted for Berkano very frequently and eventually taken out of the Younger Futhark because B and P were often substituted for one another.[17] Therefore Perth didn't make it into the Icelandic or Norwegian rune poems—all we have is the Anglo-Saxon rune poem. So when I look at Perth, I think of those unknowable things. This is the crux of divination. So often we are coming to the runes, or the tarot, or anything that we are using for divination, seeking guidance about things that we have no other way of knowing.

When Perth comes up in response to a direct question it means the runes are being purposefully vague, or there is some information that is not yours to know at this time. I think of this a lot in terms of information that other people hold that you are not supposed to know—secrets that don't pertain to you, trauma they aren't ready to share with you yet, things that are impacting their behavior in a situation that you don't need to know about.

It's not often that a diviner tells you that you aren't meant to know the answer. So when Perth comes up and it feels like a gatekeeper, it's a good idea to respect that. But it can also help to point toward what the deeper question is for you, or redirect you to ask a better question. My daily rune readings usually look like something vague, like "What do I need to know today?" When you ask the runes for something less specific, it opens them up for new interpretations and to give you the answer you need—not the one you think you need. They can show you

---

17 Crawford,"The Names of the Runes (Elder Futhark)."

something you didn't realize you needed to know. In this case, Perth isn't an evasion, but an invitation.

But enough about what Perth doesn't mean or won't tell you. What does this rune actually mean?

Most contemporary rune practitioners see Perth as connected to the gaming cup or the Well of Mímir.[18] In terms of contemporary rune practice, instead of thinking of Perth as the gaming rune, I think of it as luck. This also connects it back to the Norns again. As the ones who spin fate, they are also the ones who dole out luck. Luck was considered a part of the soul. It is an essential part of you, which means that this rune has the potential to show you how to work with this part of yourself.

The hamingja is one of the most misunderstood soul parts because it translates to "luck" or "fortune." In our modern society, we think of "luck" in very transactional terms. I think this is part of how Perth became synonymous with gambling. Yes, gambling was a very important part of pre-Christian Norse culture, but things often have double meanings, and context matters. I'm not saying that Perth can't represent gambling in the sense that we think of it today, just that the entire idea of "luck" can and should be complicated and explored for nuance.

So we inherit luck from our families, but there are also things that we can do to influence the hamingja. None of our soul parts are static—we are constantly growing, changing, and shifting, and so too are our soul parts. In his book *Spinning Wyrd*, Ryan Smith refers to the hamingja as your full ability to influence things in the world around you.[19] The hamingja is a source for manifestation and for creating the world that you want to see. But we must remember that we are not capable of controlling for every factor. Thus, people have different levels of hamingja.

Karma is a more widely understood word for the impact that previous actions have on our current lives. When I teach about the runes, one of the ways that I'm able to help students understand the concept of ørlog is through explaining it as a sort of inherited karma. Ørlog and karma are very different concepts in different cultures, but karma is

18   Mountfort, *Nordic Runes.*
19   Smith, *Spinning Wyrd.*

far more well known. The hamingja is also a sort of "karma"—in that it shifts and changes over the course of your life based on your actions.

The hamingja is sometimes personified as a female spirit, much like the dís (feminine ancestor) who supports you over the course of your life.[20] I could write a whole book about queer ancestors—and maybe someday I will!—but for those queers who are reading this and thinking "Wow, that is awfully gendered," I want to say that the important thing is that the hamingja is a nurturing spirit. It is a part of us and does not need to reflect a particular gender if that will inhibit you from connecting with it.

The hamingja is a different part of ourselves—a part that is shaped by our actions and by our values. The hamingja is connected with the rune Perth because they both signify luck. There is at the heart of this a sort of desire to control our luck, to have something personified that we can appeal to. But the wisdom of Perth is that we can't know, that some things we need to leave up to chance, and it's important to learn to be okay with that.

On a deeper level, as a queer person I look at Perth and see the process of birth and transformation. It also contains our memories, everything that we are and were, the stuff that we come from that informs who we can become. The Well of Mímir contains our memory of the ancestors. It therefore has a lot to say about our history. But the Well of Mímir also looks to the future. Once we understand the past, we have context for what we want moving forward. The future isn't set in stone, which is a huge part of what makes it unknowable. If we look forward to the future with curiosity instead of dread, it becomes a game. How do we create the best possible future for ourselves? This allows you to break free of old, repeating patterns and to move beyond dread.

This is queer Perth. This is every trans person who questioned their gender identity later in life. This is the time before you understood your sexuality, or awakened to it. It is the potential, before you fully understand and comprehend your own identity. But Perth isn't a rune of fear—it's a rune of joy, of healing. Perth welcomes you out of your chrysalis, laughing all the way.

---

20 Tauring, "Soul Parts and Healing."

Rune	Transliteration	International Phonetic Alphabet	Proto-Germanic Name	Meaning
ᛈ	p	/p/	Perth	well, luck, birth, pear tree

ANGLO-SAXON RUNE POEM:

Perth is a source of recreation and amusement to the great,
where warriors sit blithely together in the banqueting-hall.

Opportunities for Ancestral Discovery

Create an ancestor altar if you haven't already. Leave water on it. Whisper the runes into the water.

Research the Well of Mímir, and Mímir's head. The raven Muninn is also associated with memory. Clearly, memory was very important to the Old Norse. How do you see memory? How can you cultivate a better memory of where you come from?

RADICAL PERTH

- What are some things that you wish you knew, but that you can't possibly know? How can you let them go?

- What does luck mean to you? And how does luck interact with privilege? How can you cultivate more luck?

- Think about the void, the threshold of knowledge. Think about how Perth might work in tandem with Eiwaz and Jera. These three runes create Yggdrasil, time, and space. Journal about this for a while.

- Perth is connected to birth. What are you birthing right now (creative projects, art, a literal child, and so forth)? If you aren't in any birthing process, what have they been like for you in the past?

AOL/ALGIZ/ELHAZ

*Keywords: elk, awe, transformation, hunting/subsistence, being in
tune with cycles of nature, protection*

The Algiz rune is another curious rune linguistically. It's the only rune
where the sound it represents comes at the end of its name: Algiz represents "z." It is also important to note that other names for this rune
include "Elhaz," "Aol" or "Alhs." Aol doesn't even include that z sound,
and in fact this rune took on the name of Eiwaz in the Younger Futhark.
Jackson Crawford does a great job talking about this in his video on the
names of the runes from 2017.[21] The word Algiz means elk, but many
Americans would think of this animal as a moose. Because of this, I have
personal associations with this rune for independence and interdependence, as well as protection.

The shape of the rune reminds me specifically of the antlers of elk
and moose, and that shape was found in the symbol the "Helm of Aegir"
or the "Helm of Terror." This is a symbol that is found in many variations
in Scandinavian—especially Icelandic—grimoires. It's popularly used
for protection, particularly protection in battle or conflict. Each spoke at
the end of the helm of awe is shaped like Algiz from the Elder Futhark.
I have used Algiz on its own countless times in quick protection spells,
whether visualizing many Algiz runes surrounding me in a circle for personal protection or anointing a doorway or windowsill in the shape of
Algiz.

The shape of Algiz, like antlers, connects us to the wild and to the
ecstatic. Freyr is the closest in Norse tradition to a horned god. He walks
the line between the wild and the domestic, always ready to slip into
the woods. Freyr is also the one who rules over and protects the elves in

---

21   Crawford, "The Names of the Runes."

Ljosalfheim.[22] It is a realm that is parallel to ours, wild, but also beautiful. In order to live in harmony with this wild realm, we must understand and live in reciprocity with the earth. In this way, if Mannaz represents reciprocity amongst humans, Algiz represents reciprocity with nature.

Sanctuary is both a sacred space and a hallowed ground, a place where you are protected. Algiz marks the sacred. As witches we create sacred spaces where we are: we don't necessarily need a church or a temple (though those are fine spaces as well). I imagine that our ancestors would have had to do the same thing, especially as people were migrating and traveling long distances. Of course there were the sacred groves of home, but you still needed to create that space on the move. This brings to mind the migratory patterns of reindeer and the people (mostly Sámi) who traveled with them. To this day Sámi people are still seminomadic, still following the reindeer. There is a powerful connection here, one where the reindeer participate in cultural preservation just as the Sámi participate in preserving reindeer herds. This is what I mean by mutual reciprocity.

Many rune workers also see this rune as a rune of the hunt—especially when paired with Eiwaz or Uruz or both. But it's not just hunting in the woods blindly, it's also about cultivation and living as a part of the ecosystem. This is a part of our lives and role that we have taken too far: humans take from the world without balance. Carnivores and omnivores are an essential part of the ecosystem, but it's important to work with and not against it, lest we destroy that which protects us. Kari Tauring talks about the deep connection between the Sámi peoples and the reindeer.[23] The Sámi follow the reindeer. They let the reindeer and elk lead, and follow them where they go. The Sámi also teach us that it's important to maintain a climate and environment where the reindeer can thrive. So it's not about taking everything—it is also about preserving systems so that they can survive.

This is a rune with the great potential for protection—particularly for rural living and transmasc/gender nonconforming queers. I think it is particularly interesting that this rune took on the name of Eiwaz

---

22 Kvilhaug, *Seed of Yggdrasil.*
23 Tauring, *The Runes.*

later in runic history. Of course, the runes have changed a great deal in meaning over the years. I think it's actually helpful to trace some of these transformations—particularly when we are looking at them from an unabashedly contemporary perspective. There is an aspect to this rune of transformation and journey work, especially when combined with Eiwaz. This transformation can be literal—gender transition, coming out, and other physical manifestations of internal transitions. But it can also be really helpful in spiritual life—particularly for those who enter a sort of "other space" through trance and journey work. Algiz acts as the protective rune while Eiwaz is the rune to use for journeying.

You can also use Algiz as a magical warning system. Invoking Algiz will help you be aware if you need to move on, to be alert to danger. The idea of protection in and of itself implies that you need to be protected from something. Incorporating this rune into your home's wards will help you to intuitively feel when something is off or you need to adjust the wards.

Algiz can hallow queer spaces just as well as any other space, in particular, the connection between the mind, body, and soul that comes with using this rune to create sacred space. Use Algiz to help you connect with your inner self. This rune is an assistant as you are trying to figure out who you are. It acts as a sort of protection that will allow you to explore your identity in a safe way. If this is a rune of creating space, allow it to cocoon you so you have the space to figure out the answers to big questions about your own gender and sexuality.

And once those questions are answered, this rune can also continue to help you as you find safety and security in your community. It is suitable protection for both individuals and groups. It is that aspect of both protecting and hallowing at once—it helps us to carve out safe spaces for our internal worlds at the same time that it helps us to create safe spaces among our own worlds. Algiz can help us to protect our personal lives—both behind closed doors and in the community. This rune can also help to protect us when we go into "battle"—especially when paired with Eiwaz, Sowilo, and Isa. This is a good rune to help us stick to our beliefs and principles when we need to fight to create a life for ourselves in the world.

Rune	Transliteration	International Phonetic Alphabet	Proto-Germanic Name	Meaning
ᛉ	z	/z/	Algiz	elk, protection, defense

ANGLO-SAXON RUNE POEM:

The Eolh-sedge is mostly to be found in a marsh;
it grows in the water and makes a ghastly wound,
covering with blood every warrior who touches it.

Opportunities for Ancestral Discovery

Did you ever go hunting with your family? What sorts of traditions or rituals did your family have around the hunt?

What are the hunting seasons in your area? What wildlife are hunted, and what do those particular wildlife mean to you? What wildlife would your ancestors have hunted?

RADICAL ALGIZ

- What does the word "hunt" mean to you? Think both literally and archetypically.

- What are you seeking? What are you personally hunting right now? How can that hunt be incorporated into your own spiritual practice?

- What makes a space sacred for you?

- How can you seek more sacred spaces? How can you build sacred space into your own life now?

- Create an amulet of Algiz, and wear it around your neck or tucked in your pocket. Journal any outcomes here.

SOWILO

Keywords: Sunna, sun, victory, success

Sowilo is the rune of the sun. It is shining down upon us, determining the gravitational pull of the Earth. Without the sun we are unable to live life as we do now. The Norse assigned the sun to a Goddess: Sunna. She drives her golden chariot across the sky, pulled by her two horses Arvak (early-wakener) and Alsvith (all-strong).[24] Her brother is Mani, the Moon God. The Norse often find balance by pairing male and female deities: while the Moon God is Mani, the Goddess of Night is Nott, and the God of Day is Dag while the Sun Goddess is Sunna. There is another rune specifically for Day, which we will cover in the next Ætt.

Unfortunately, many of you might recognize this rune from its association with the Nazis. The Nazis used two of this rune next to each other as the logo for their Secret Service. They were known for running the concentration camps. For this reason, I never place two Sowilos next to each other in a bindrune, and nor should you. Of course, the Nazis chose to use this rune in particular because it is a herald of victory and power (and it looks almost exactly like S, which make it the initials of the SS).

But this is deeply twisted, a wound that we need to work actively to heal.

When I read about Sowilo, it is ultimately healing to read about the feminine side of the sun. Sunna is beautiful and caring, and brings us vital life force. She is strength to find the right path, and ultimately a beacon of survival. Sunna is most powerful at the solstices: winter, because if she refuses to return, we're all fucked. And she's powerful at the summer solstice because that is when she is at the height of her

---

24   Kvilhaug, *The Seed of Yggdrasill.*

power. She is divine cosmic energy, weaving together what we need to survive and—somehow—making it beautiful.

There is room for many others who are gender-nonconforming within the feminine and masculine areas, but when we're looking at the mythology we need to look at them as metaphors and ideas. As I've talked about earlier, Maria Kvilhaug talks about gender as a metaphor in her seminal work *The Seed of Yggdrasill*.[25] And if gender is a metaphor, then it is an abstract concept and should not be used to limit the lives of queer people off the page. Personally, as a gender-fluid person I find thinking about gender as a metaphor to be really interesting because I know that there are times when I feel like I'm on one side of a binary, but I don't know what femininity or masculinity really are or mean and the answer is: they don't have set meanings. What femininity and masculinity represent is much more interesting to me.

But! All of that is to say that Sowilo is an unusually gendered rune. For those who have bought into the patriarchy, success is often synonymous with men and masculinity. Neoconservatives try to convince others that career success is for men, and that success in the home is for women. But when we understand this mythological gender swap from the (modern, American) idea that the sun is masculine and the moon is feminine, we open up to possibilities. Chances are, you see both (and all) genders in the sun. Which means that this is not a harsh, toxic masculine understanding of success that leaves out anyone who isn't a cis man. This is instead an understanding of success that is much more nurturing, allowing for success in the boardroom, the garden, the family, the small business, the artist.

My Sowilo is not the rune of toxic masculinity. It is the rune of the sun goddess, amber, golden light in the afternoon. It is the light that shines on the painter's canvas just as much as it is the light that grows vegetables in the summer.

Sowilo is a powerful sign of manifestation. Tauring makes the distinction that this is the power *to* manifest, not the manifestation itself.[26]

---

25 Kvilhaug, *The Seed of Yggdrasill*.
26 Tauring, *The Runes*.

Sowilo is a blessing. It helps us figure out our passions and carry our creative projects through to completion. Sowilo connects the darkness and the light. This might not make sense, but when you put yourself in the mindset of the Norse, there are really two halves of the year: dark and light, winter and summer. The sun provides guidance and is the most important celestial body for time-tracking in this sense.

Of course, it wouldn't be a Norse story of the sun without themes of rebirth. This is especially close to my heart. We work so hard to become ourselves, to recognize who we are. Then, it takes courage to bring that self forward. Sowilo gives us the courage to be who we are. This is another one of those themes that comes up over and over again for me as I write my way through the runes.

I think too often that people in heathen and Nordic spaces can get bogged down by forcing themselves into really strict ideas of ancestor veneration. It would be so easy to make this a spiritual space of repeating the mistakes of our ancestors over and over again in an attempt to venerate them. And to an extent, that is exactly what happened with the Icelandic sagas. We see here that blood debts were passed on from one generation to the next, which did not lead to good things for the family. But it is also precisely these kinds of successes that get written down—the successes that are also ultimately a failure. To be a successful murderer is not truly success in the way that I read Sowilo. This is a rune of nurturing success, after all. It is a rune of the growing season, of allowing the plants to unfurl without the stress of winter. There is hard work to be done, yes. But it is the hard work of making life work.

Of course the shape of this rune means I associate it almost immediately with Thor—which is very funny because the sun isn't out when rain and thunder are rolling through the landscape. However, Thor is widely understood to have been a very agrarian and farming god. As the god in charge of the weather, he was the one that many prayed to in order to ensure that the crops came in. Now, in a time of a warming planet, Thor is the god I pray to during the droughts of summer. Please, continue to bring your rain to our land. And so of course when we think of other things our ancestors would have been preoccupied with during the sunny side of the year, we think of this great agrarian work.

Rune	Transliteration	International Phonetic Alphabet	Proto-Germanic Name	Meaning
ᛊᛋ	s	/s/	Sowilo	sun, victory

ANGLO-SAXON RUNE POEM:

> The sun is ever a joy in the hopes of seafarers
> when they journey away over the fishes' bath,
> until the courser of the deep bears them to land.

ICELANDIC RUNE POEM:

> Sun
> shield of the clouds
> and shining ray
> and destroyer of ice.

NORWEGIAN RUNE POEM:

> Sun is the light of the world;
> I bow to the divine decree.

Opportunities for Ancestral Discovery

"Hail the Day"

These are stanzas 2–4 of Sigrdrífumál.[27] It is a fragment of pagan prayer, sung by the Valkyrie Sigrdrífa after she has awoken.

---

27 "Sigrdrífumál," in Larrington, *The Poetic Edda*.

Heill dagr
heilir dags synir
heil nott oc nipt
oreiþom gom
litiþ ocr þinig
oc gefit sitiondom sigr

#

Heilir ęsir
heilar asynior
heil sia in fiolnyta fold
mal oc manvit
gefit ocr męrom tveim
oc lęcnishendr meþan lifom

And my translation:

Hail, Day!
Hail, sons of Day!
Hail, Night and her daughters!
Look down upon us with kind eyes
And grant us victory

#

Hail, the gods,
Hail, the goddesses,
And all the generous earth!
Give us wisdom, and impeccable word
And healing hands for our life-long.

For your ancestor exercise, set an alarm to wake up before dawn. Sit at your altar, and wait for the day to break. Recite either the Norse or my translation of the prayer. Notice how it feels.

RADICAL SOWILO

- Look up sun motifs and art. What does the sun mean to you?
  What do these depictions stir in you?

- Think about the winter and summer solstices. Think about
  any moods, emotions, anniversaries, or traditions you have
  around those days. How could you bring some more solar
  worship into your own traditions?

Sunna Spritz Recipe

Create a Norse solar essence!

Materials:
Birch bark or leaves
Sunflower petals
Cedar
Mugwort
Marigold
*A clear quartz crystal (or any other rock that resonates with you
     that isn't harmful!)*

Place all ingredients for your solar essence in a jar. Pour warm water (*not*
boiling but almost) over them. Place the jar in the sun to charge.

When it has charged for a specific amount of time, sift the herbs out
of the water. Add brandy in equal parts.

You can use your spritz to invigorate yourself, shift the energy in
your space for the better, or to start your day on the right track.

6

The Third Ætt

TYR/TIWAZ

Keywords: Tyr, justice, balance, shild, the future

Tyr is a god of justice. He is known as the guiding star, the one who shows us how to act with honor. Snorri Sturluson associated Tyr with war and victory in the *Prose Edda*. When Tyr shows up as a god of justice, it is specifically as a god of justice as decided by war and conflict. He is a god of great principle, who tries to see things in as true a light as possible and figure out what is right and fair. He is supposed to be a god who is impeccable with his word, dedicated to speaking the truth even when that truth is ugly.

But even Tyr has the ability to betray his own values. In the myth of the Fenriswolf, Tyr is the central player—and this is the main story that we have of him. I particularly love Neil Gaiman's adaptation of the story.[1] The story goes that, even as a puppy, Fenrir was becoming diffi-

---

1   Gaiman, *Norse Mythology*.

cult to manage. The Aesir decided they needed to bind him. They challenged him to a "game," betting that he could break free of any chain they used to bind him. He takes them up on their bet, tail wagging and teeth gnashing. The gods promise to release him if he is truly caught by the chain. Out of mutual respect, he asks that one of the gods hold their hand in his mouth. If he is not released, he has the right to bite that god's hand off. Tyr offers his hand, and when Fenrir is bound, he bites off the hand in revenge and anger.

Tyr was the god who was willing to pay the price for deception. This may have been considered a necessary deception, but even so it was not right. This is an example of Tyr paying shild. This is an old Norse concept of debt, obligation, or even necessary action. When someone hurts someone else, they need to pay shild in order to make things right. The Old Norse word "shild" is associated with the word "Skuld," which you might recognize as the Norn of the future. She does not truly represent the "future," but what should be—if you act in accordance with your values. This story is one of the most important stories that I know to represent and understand the concept of shild. It's not an eye for an eye—it is a sacrifice that is made that is equal to the wrong done. But shild is also an important way of keeping the peace. The bloody family sagas that have been handed down show the consequences of not paying appropriate shild.[2]

From the perspective of community justice, once the reparation has been made, you need to be able to move on. This is another lesson of the family sagas we have left over from the Middle Ages. Tyr's sacrifice of his hand is that reparation—but it doesn't meet the full requirement for justice, as Fenrir's continued imprisonment is a deep injustice and betrayal. This is why Fenrir fights with his father Loki against the gods in Ragnarök, and how he ultimately kills Odin.

Paying shild is something I think about a lot in terms of abolition. As I'm thinking again about the binding of the Fenriswolf, the more I realize that Tyr's sacrifice of his hand is not actually appropriate shild. Prison in itself is a deep, deep injustice that Fenrir faces. Tyr becomes

---

2   Kellogg, *The Sagas of Icelanders*.

comfortable without his hand, but Fenrir's anger only deepens. Tyr paid exactly what he said he would, keeping his word, but this is a funda-mental show that the gods at this point in the mythos have failed their own ethics. They are trying desperately to cover their own hubris, their own corruption at this point in the cycles. To the abolitionist, Loki and Fenrir and all the others who were chained are heroes who break free from their chains.

I've written many times over in this book that if I were to write the story of the cosmological poems from the *Poetic Edda* into one giant story, it would be a story of fall from grace, and what it takes to rebuild. The story feels like the lessons learned from past gods—or maybe future ones. The great drama is demonstrating how not to be, the kind of pride and actions not to take. This stands in stark contrast to how divin-ity is portrayed in other—more modern—religions. The Christian god is intended to be omniscient, all-powerful, a culmination of all that is good and wise in the world. So when that god takes actions that are spiteful in the Old Testament, or when Jesus himself takes spiteful actions, it is read more often as a just punishment than a reprehensible action taken in a moment of weakness on the god's part.

There are other paganisms and pantheons that feel similar—Greco-Roman myth in particular comes to mind. I never connected much with Hellenic mythology, and I think a big part of that was that the first time I was really introduced to the pantheon it was in stories of Hercules and Zeus, stories in which the retellings did Hera dirty and treated her like a shrew for being displeased with Zeus's (very bad) behavior. Even as a child I knew it was misogynistic before I knew what that word meant. Of course, this is because of the particular retellings that I ate up as a kid, and I'm certain there are many Hellenic pagans who would disagree with me. But I do think it's important to talk about the ways that old gods take on a more instructive quality than omniscient creator gods.

Whenever justice comes up in divination, I am always reminded that what I believe to be right is not always what is just. Runes or cards of justice often indicate an imbalance and the need to bring things back into balance. Sometimes we need to read them literally, and when Tiwaz comes up it often indicates a legal problem or conflict that needs to be resolved.

Rune	Transliteration	International Phonetic Alphabet	Proto-Germanic Name	Meaning
↑	t	/t/	Tiwaz	justice, the god Tyr

ANGLO-SAXON RUNE POEM:

Tiw is a guiding star; well does it keep faith with princes;
it is ever on its course over the mists of night and never fails.

ICELANDIC RUNE POEM:

Týr
god with one hand
and leavings of the wolf
and prince of temples.

NORWEGIAN RUNE POEM:

Tyr is a one-handed god;
often has the smith to blow.

Opportunities for Ancestral Discovery

Were there any famous court cases—or even villains—in your ancestry? What was the outcome, and what would justice have looked like?

RADICAL TIWAZ

- What does justice mean to you?

- Where do you see injustice happening? Journal about this. Now, take some time and pick out where you actually have power to fight the injustice. Make a (doable!) commitment.

- What reparations do you need to make, and what is the best way to make them?

- How can you bring things back into balance?

BERKANA/BERKANO

Keywords: birch tree, healing, creativity, pregnancy, in process

Berkano is another tree rune, this time a rune of deep healing. The birch is an incredibly important plant in Norse folk medicine. It places us in a specific place (above the 45th parallel), and it holds an important place in the cultures of people who live above the birch line. For Nordic people, the birch is associated with pregnancy, birth, and all significant life passages.

Part of the birch tree's focus as a healing tree is in how many different things we can do with it. The bark itself is waterproof and rot-resistant, and makes for good basket material or even "paper." The sod roofs you'll see across Scandinavia all have birchbark underneath them, keeping the rain out. Birch sap is sweet and often tapped for use in sweets. Birch oil itself—the essential oil that comes from birch—is medicinal, antiseptic. Around the tree, mushrooms often grow. Chaga is a mushroom used as an adaptogen and all-around immune booster, called kreftkjuke in Norway (Cancer fungus) after its anticarcinogenic properties. It will help to boost the energy and the immune system. *Amanita muscaria* also grows along the birch, which is a mushroom traditionally used for its psychedelic properties to aid in spirit flight. The birch tree itself supports a whole ecosystem that the Norse ancestors worked with for healing and spirituality.

I think it's fascinating that both of the tree runes in the Elder Futhark have anticarcinogenic properties in real life. Both trees are used in both allopathic and naturopathic medicine. They are twins—Eiwaz showing the portal to death and the underworld, and Berkano showing the portal to birth and healing. Each rune works well with the other, not two sides of a binary but rather partners.

Berkano, the rune itself, is connected to a tree that has grown in symbiosis with Nordic peoples. It signifies birth (and rebirth), healing, and creativity. When used with Ingwaz (coming up later), we have a potent combination of runes for all forms of creativity—but of course Berkano can help with that all on its own. It's important to me that we recognize the connection here between creativity and healing. Finding creative expression is like finding a resource within yourself. When I am personally expressing myself creatively, it means that I have the bravery in my heart to put something out into the world. And sometimes creativity helps you work through turbulent times—there are countless examples of this, from Frida Kahlo's painting through her chronic pain to Taylor Swift exorcising her breakup emotions through songwriting. From the perspective of personal creativity, Berkano helps you maintain consistency—like journaling every day. Your creative work does not need to be devoured by an audience in order to be important to you. The very process of creativity is an alchemy in and of itself.

In *Lessons from the Empress* (coauthored with Cassandra Snow) we wrote about divorcing the creativity of the Empress tarot card from outdated concepts of motherhood. Often the Empress card includes a woman either with a child or heavily pregnant. Cassandra and I used the Empress as a jumping-off point to discuss creativity itself, and in doing so opened the generative quality of the archetype up beyond "production of children." I want to do this with Berkano as well! Berkano is less viscerally associated with motherhood because this is a letter, not an artistic representation on a card. However there are a lot of rune readers and writers who associate Berkano with pregnancy—if you squint it looks like a person with breasts and a large belly from the side.

Of course, this is not to discount the importance of motherhood or parenthood. Pregnancy is a beautiful and challenging part of life, and childrearing is sacred. But too often mothers get boxed into this stereotype that their creativity and production should be about their children. I disagree with this cultural assumption, and I want to carve out space within Berkano to allow for creativity to expand beyond childbearing and rearing. It is possible (and even necessary!) for parents to have outlets for creativity and play that are outside the lives of their children. I do not have children myself, but this is something that I hear consistently from my parent friends.

Some of the most iconic folk rituals of Scandinavia are the sauna rituals. A sauna can reach intense heat, which keeps the space sterile. You can cook on the sauna stove and sleep on the benches (when the sauna heat isn't going, obviously). Birch oil is often added to the bucket of water for steam in saunas, cleansing the air. Some of the best-known sauna rituals involve a birch whisk for cleansing the skin, which is birch twigs with leaves on them tied together and brushed across the skin. This helps to improve circulation and clears away dead skin. Dead bodies were prepared in sauna in Finland, because—again—it could be kept at such a hot temperature and the steam could keep you safe. The sauna is a moment of transformation, of resurrection, and reinvigoration.

So Berkano is a rune to work with when you are working with big life transitions: a move, a birth in the family, a death in the family. It is deeply healing and calls you into stillness in an incredible way. One of the ways that the tree spirit of this rune speaks to me is through the utter stillness and hope that I feel in a birch grove. There is a sort of lightness that lives just under the ribcage. Emily Dickinson wasn't kidding—and that thing with feathers is something I feel in the presence of Birch. Without hope in the picture, it's hard to find the courage to create and put my work out in the world.

From a queer perspective, Berkano can help us to find found family. It is a rune of connection as much as it is about creation. Throughout this passage I have continuously referred to it as being in partnership with other runes, which shows off the communal aspect of this rune. This rune could also be a very beautiful rune for queer parents to work with. Berkano has a gentle and accepting energy that can help you to learn what parenting out of the cis-straight norm means for you. You could also utilize the energy of this rune (paired with Othila or other runes) to help with fostering, adoption, IVF, or any other queer child-rearing shellwork.

Rune	Transliteration	International Phonetic Alphabet	Proto-Germanic Name	Meaning
ᛒ	b	/b/	Berkano	birch tree

ANGLO-SAXON RUNE POEM:

The poplar bears no fruit; yet without seed it brings forth suckers,
for it is generated from its leaves.
Splendid are its branches and gloriously adorned
its lofty crown which reaches to the skies.

ICELANDIC RUNE POEM:

Birch
leafy twig
and little tree
and fresh young shrub.

NORWEGIAN RUNE POEM:

Birch has the greenest leaves of any shrub;
Loki was fortunate in his deceit.

Opportunities for Ancestral Discovery

Did your ancestors come from the "birch line" (45th parallel north)? What would they have used birch for?

Research the sauna and sauna rituals. If possible, go to a sauna and chant Berkano under your breath several times. See if you can feel any energy shift or change.

RADICAL BERKANO

- Many of the healing runes are connected with trees, or with seeds. What are some associations you've had with trees?

- Think about the last time you went through a significant life passage. Now look at the rituals associated with Birch. How could you have used this medicine in your past?

- Look into the properties of Chaga. Does this seem like an herb that would be helpful for you? I definitely don't recommend taking herbs when you don't need them, but learning more about this medicine could also help others.

EHWAZ

Keywords: horse, travel, familiar, cooperation, group mentality

Rune of the horse, Ehwaz is connected to travel. The horse and travel were both massive parts of Old Norse culture. There are so many named horses in the myths, showing the importance of human-equine relationships. There are stanzas in the *Hávamál* that speak to how travel is essential for understanding the truth of the world. There is within this rune a deep sense of wanderlust. Odin himself is well known in the archetype of the Wanderer. Sleipnir, Odin's horse, has eight legs and is able to travel farther distances than a normal horse. Sleipnir moves easily between the worlds and is even able to leap over the wall of fire in Hel's land.

Horses were the primary creature used for travel by land by the Germanic and Old Norse. This is extremely important to bear in mind as we approach this rune. In the *Hávamál*, or the Sayings of the High One, there are many verses that talk about the necessity of travel to gain wisdom. There are deep restlessness and wanderlust within the Norse mythos. The Allfather is the Wanderer, not the King who stays in his hall to watch over the comings and goings of his kingdom. Odin gains wisdom from moving far and wide, talking to everyone he comes across. The act of travel itself is seen as holy. The horse is a vehicle and a guide, mythic, beautiful.

There's a reason a lot of the famous high-fantasy books are journeying narratives. The act of movement creates a liminal space in which magical workings can occur. Within Norse folk magic tradition, if you are going on a walk to gain insight (a divination practice called the Årsgång), everyone you meet along the way is a potential sign.[3] Horses

---

3   Gårdbäck, *Trolldom.*

and humans have a very interesting relationship. Horses are incredibly intelligent creatures, who get to know humans who work with them on a deep, intimate level. Most other esoteric rune workers talk about how this rune can be a kenning for good working relationships. I see this as trust. The horse must trust the rider, and the rider must trust the horse, in order for the relationship to work. Each one must bring something important to the table, and each looks after the other.

We don't need to have these same relationships with our vehicles today. I can't imagine having any sort of "trust" for a car. We've lost this aspect of travel. That's not a terrible thing—sometimes we just evolve and technology moves on. And that is definitely one way to think of the relationship between humans and horses: technology.

The ability of people to interact with and train horses for things like tilling the field as well as things like battle meant that things changed dramatically. To a people who were introduced to horses, this relationship meant that they were able to do so much more than before. It dramatically changed their lives and civilizations.

There are still people who work with horses, but we are no longer in as close a symbiotic relationship.

When I think of the archetype of the horse in terms of leftist movements, I think about the process of building a collective. Working together toward a new vision takes a lot of trust, and it's easy to move through this step quickly. I know that at least when I'm working as an activist, I want to get into the work and figure out how I can be most useful. But it's important to take that time, to make sure that our visions are aligned and that we trust each other. When we take that time, it allows us to move in symbiosis with others; it allows us to work as a unit.

Ehwaz is also a rune that signifies change—but it is a change that you have an active part in. Yes, the horse symbolizes travel, but horses were also used in battle and tending the farm. The horse is an active partner in these activities. Therefore, the horse was instrumental in making change happen. Whether you are tilling a field or going to battle, the horse is a vehicle to keep you moving forward. We must honor the horses as the agents of change and movement that they are.

This rune is not just about the horse itself, but also about our relationship to the horse as well as the ability to work in close tandem with another person or team. We may not often have the ability to interact with horses in our everyday lives, but that necessity of teamwork is still very much there. Our teams just look different now. We have designated workspaces outside of the home/farm/immediate family. We also have people that we are in activist community with and who need our love and care as we build a new world together.

Ehwaz helps us to understand how to form better working relationships with others. There are other runes in the Futhark that are good for working on relationships with family and lovers, but this is so much more about work collaborations and community outside of your chosen family. It is said that horses develop a psychic connection with their rider—this is a sentiment that I know not from science, but from the people in my life who have worked closely with horses.

For the queer rune reader, the horse has another really important aspect: its connection with Loki. Loki is the mother (birthing parent) of Sleipnir, the eight-legged horse that Odin rides to get between the worlds. Perhaps Sleipnir is able to transcend the boundaries between the worlds because Sleipnir's primary parent was a trickster, a shape-shifting god. This is also one of the stories in which Loki's gender-bending is incredibly important. I am of course talking about the myth of the unnamed builder that agreed to build a wall around Valhalla in three seasons in exchange for Freyja, the sun, and the moon. The gods didn't believe that the builder could possibly finish the wall in the given time. However, the builder had a horse named Svaðilfari that moved at a supernatural speed, and it looked like he would finish by the end of the cycle. Freyja was rightly upset that the gods had so casually offered her up as a prize, and they knew they had to do something. Loki transformed into a mare and tempted the builder's stallion to run away with her. Loki did not return for some time, and without his precious steed, the builder was not able to finish the wall on time. Later, Loki returned with a young foal with eight legs. This horse was the best horse among gods and men. In their form as a mare, Loki is both playful and protective of their community—and themselves.

Depending on the retelling that you read, Loki is either afraid of the gods' revenge or they are simply bailing them out of a bad deal. Some would say that it was Loki's smooth talking that got the gods to agree to the deal in the first place. In these versions of the story, the gods angrily turn against Loki when they are about to have to pay. Loki then distracts Svaðilfari in order to save their own skin. But in some retellings, you could look at it as Loki working to find creative solutions for the gods' problems.

If Sleipnir is the best horse, the prototypical horse, the one that we measure other horses against for their loyalty and talents, then Sleipnir's beginnings as the result of queer shape-shifting are something we must pay attention to. This is a potent moment for queer play and joy—and also working together to create something queer. Maybe that means working in some kind of collaborative art, like theater, but it could also mean infusing your activist work with more fun. Finding ways to make the process of building a new world collaborative and visionary is important.

Ehwaz is almost the Mannaz rune—all you need to do is complete the two lines of the top of the "m" shape and you get Mannaz (ᛗ). It is no surprise then that Mannaz is the next rune in our progression.

Rune	Transliteration	International Phonetic Alphabet	Proto-Germanic Name	Meaning
ᛖ	e	/e(:)/	Ehwaz	horse

ANGLO-SAXON RUNE POEM:

The horse is a joy to princes in the presence of warriors.
A steed in the pride of its hoofs,
when rich men on horseback bandy words about it;
and it is ever a source of comfort to the restless.

Opportunities for Ancestral Discovery

Many of our ancestors—no matter the culture—kept horses. When's the most recent instance of your family keeping horses? What is the story there? What was your family's relationship to horses?

Has your family traveled widely? What is your present-day relationship to travel? What might ancestral traveling have looked like for you?

RADICAL EHWAZ

- What does travel mean for you? Take some time to think about any wisdom you've gained traveling, and how that has shifted your life.

- Have you ever ridden a horse? What was the experience like? If possible, find a way to connect with a horse. If that's not possible, watch some videos about horses. Learn about their intelligence and connect with their spirit.

- How can you create a better sense of symbiosis in your projects, or at work? What are some team-building techniques you could use? Are there any places where your team may need healing?

MANNAZ

Keywords: humanity, community, reciprocity,
providing for one another

This is one of my favorite runes. It means humanity, people working together to create supportive communities. This is one of the most important runes in my own practice, particularly around working with chosen family. What we do to create connection matters. So many people who practice folk magic are solitary practitioners, and a lot of pagans I know aren't terribly interested in working in a coven or don't have the resources to work with others in a magical setting.

This rune is very personal to me. It's hard for me to write about Mannaz without drawing on my own personal experiences in community. Mannaz is about sharing your gifts and delighting in the gifts of others, and as a professional diviner/oracle/witch/writer, the things that I share with the community are deeply personal.

A lot of the runes aren't necessarily about the deep, dark magic we do in private. They aren't about complicated rituals, or the secrets of the universe. They're more about what we do with our lives in this moment, how we relate to one another and the mythos we love. They are wisdom, yes, but utterly practical. They are the grandmother wisdom that you collect from baking bread with her.

Mannaz is definitely this way. I see it as a rune about how we are meant to relate to one another: in an open, trusting, and reciprocal way. We are meant to give and take in equity, to make sure that we all have what we need. In this way Mannaz is an aspirational rune. If we are not able to communicate openly like this now, this rune challenges us to ask how we can communicate more in the future.

Many rune workers look at this rune and they can see two people, arms outstretched, coming together in an embrace. You could also see two figures handing one another gifts. This makes sense to me as well, because we're looking at two staves with a gyfu connecting them. Mannaz is therefore connected with Gyfu: humanity and the gifts we give one another. This is a rune of beautiful interdependence.

But this rune also stores important cultural and historic knowledge: as a rune of mankind, working with this runic spirit can help us understand our collective human memory. This can also indicate any questions of identity in a reading, what it means to be human specifically. Mountfort reads this rune as instruction to work with your talents to better humanity as a whole. He connects it to an idea of the evolution of humanity—of how we have evolved spiritually over the generations and how we can continue to lift each other up.[4]

I also read this rune as a reminder of the joys that can be had in community. This is going to the queer club and dancing your ass off in a safe space. This is a knitting circle with your favorite people. This is long book-club brunches with a close-knit group of friends. Mannaz is also about making it up to others when you have harmed them—as we can see in the Anglo-Saxon rune poem. It is growing together.

It's important to think of Mannaz in the context of coming right after Ehwaz. In the previous rune we learned how to work together toward a shared vision, and now we're bringing that vision to the rest of our community. Mannaz is a bit more of a refinement, an aspirational rune. The deeper into the Futhark we get the more aspirational runes we come across.

When this rune is haunting you, it is time to consider your relationship to the community at large. Are you in right relationship? Do you need to give more of yourself? Are you giving too much and do you need to get better at receiving support from your community?

I first started writing this book before the pandemic, continued it during, and now I am finishing it in post-lockdown life. My relationship to community has shifted throughout those times. Of course during the pandemic one of the best things that I could do to care for the community was to stay separated from other people. Maintaining a distance

---

4   Mountfort, *Nordic Runes.*.

was necessary, even as it felt like it was most important to show up and be there for family. That was one of the things that was most challenging for me—I'm used to being a person who shows up. The pandemic forced a boundary upon people in a really essential way, and now we are attempting to figure out what that means for us. Mannaz is not only the connection between people, but it is also the necessary boundaries that are needed to keep relationships healthy. You can look at Mannaz as a Gyfu suspended between two Isas—the gift held up by boundaries.

Mannaz also helps us understand not just the way some relationships are but also the way relationships ought to be. It can be difficult to figure out what kind of relationships you want to have if good relationships weren't modeled for you early on. If you grew up in a household where your parents were constantly arguing, where they didn't have shared values and treated one another more as enemies than partners—then it will be very difficult to figure out what a healthy relationship is for you. If you were bullied as a child for being different, it might mean that you have trust issues or attachment issues. The same goes if you were the one doing the bullying.

That's why I think that conceiving of Mannaz as a healthy, boundaries relationship is necessary. Boundaries are compassionate toward yourself and the people that you're in relationship with, in spite of our potential feelings about those boundaries. In *The Runes: A Deeper Journey*, Kari Tauring discusses Mannaz as a rune where the strong are protecting and supporting the members of the community who need it the most.[5] It's the strong people on the outside of the rune, holding up the youth and the elders. Mannaz means a holy enclosure made up of the arms of loved ones. There is a sense of support here.

When Mannaz is present in your life, you might not even realize it. You may be feeling uplifted by any time that you spend with your loved ones, or perhaps if you're introverted you may not be feeling as drained by being around others. You have struck a balance that works for both you and the people around you. This is intentional connection at its best.

---

5   Tauring, *The Runes.*

We need to be able to recognize the people who support us no matter what, those people who are holding us up when things are bad and when things are good. This web of community needs to be strong enough to withstand dire threats. In spite of what capitalism would have us believe, we do still need one another. No one can get through this life alone, completely self-sustained. Humans are social animals. Mannaz is then a recognition of family.

Queer people have found ways over the centuries of recognizing one another. It could be the slang, the way someone talks, a haircut, symbols that they wear. This is the recognition of the violet as a sapphic symbol for Victorians/Edwardians. It's knowing that you could go to certain bars and be allowed to exist. It's having our own slang, even "gay voice." All of these are ways to signal to new people that we are in the life.

Rune	Transliteration	International Phonetic Alphabet	Proto-Germanic Name	Meaning
ᛗ	m	/m/	Mannaz	man/humankind

ANGLO-SAXON RUNE POEM:

The joyous man is dear to his kinsmen;
yet every man is doomed to fail his fellow,
since the Lord by his decree will commit the vile carrion to the earth.

ICELANDIC RUNE POEM:

Man
delight of man
and augmentation of the earth
and adorner of ships.

NORWEGIAN RUNE POEM:

Man is an augmentation of the dust;
great is the claw of the hawk.

Opportunities for Ancestral Discovery

The Norwegian and Icelandic rune poems both talk about Mannaz as an augmentation of the earth. I read this as humans working together to tend the earth. In what ways were your ancestors in relationship with the land?

What does memory mean to you, when you think of ancestors? How can you bring ancestor memory into more of your daily life?

RADICAL MANNAZ

- How do you define community?

- What does your community look like? Are there any ways you want to shift your community?

- What does it feel like to be held by community? How do you receive support?

- Think about your talents. How can you use your talents to give back to your community?

LAGUZ

Keywords: lake, leek, water, magic, herbalism

Laguz, the lake, the leek, depth of meaning, sorcery. This is a beautiful rune for any creative person, especially poets and fine artists. There are many different mystical systems that see water as a generating, healing force. It is a source of creativity, of life passages, of our relationships with one another. This even makes sense scientifically, thinking back to the water creatures that all life evolved from. We started in water and end in earth or fire.

Water was a very important element in Old Norse culture. Obviously, they were a seafaring people, and that is reflected in the rune poems. The ocean is talked about with respect and also fear. I almost read the Anglo-Saxon rune poem as a challenge: if you are not brave, do not venture into the unknown depths of the ocean, even in a ship. It's something that you need to steel yourself for. There's a sort of cosmic depth to this rune.

Water is often associated with healing magic. But that does not mean that water is a soft element: it forms ice. A storm at sea can down a ship, and doldrums at sea can also slaughter a full ship of people slowly through starvation. When we associate this rune with the ocean, we plunge into a dangerous mystery. Roughly 95 percent of the ocean remains unexplored by modern scientists. What secrets does this water hold?

The ocean, the fjords, the rivers—all of these held a dear place in the cosmology of the ancestors. Rán is the goddess of the ocean, and she is a death goddess as much as she is a healing goddess. Rán has a huge net that she uses to capture the dead who fall from ships and are buried at sea. Rán has nine daughters, who bring light to the spirits that live in the ocean. Njörðr the god of the sea also has nine daughters—they are giantesses who are described as rune carvers and weavers. They do their work in the underworld, where they welcome souls ready to receive the judgment of the Norns.[6]

This connection between water and the underworlds and death shows us that this creates a space between life and death, a place where the knife's edge of healing or dying is felt deeply. In water our bodies float, suspended between the realms. This is also an important thing to consider for one of the most potent forms of magic known in the Norse world: seiðr.

Seiðr is the art of a trance-based magical practice that includes blessings, curses, and prophecy. Linguistically the word "seiðr" is thought to come from two different areas: an ancestor of the English word "to seethe," as well as the Old Norse word "sed," which evolves into the words "sit" and "set." Seething connects to the great churning well of Hvergelmir, the spring in Niflhel whence all waters rise. It is deeply connected with water, flow, and even the danger that you can encounter being in water. I think of "seething" in the same breath as "churning," and it evokes the image of water rushing over my head as I'm pulled under the tide. At first glance, "sit" isn't as sexy an etymological root. But my training in Nordic folk magic has taught me that "sitting out" is actually a very important practice magically speaking—and it is even an initiatory practice.

Útiseta is the art of sitting out in Nordic folk magic. The magician undertakes útisetning in order to gain more power and talents in the magical arts. As with a lot of Nordic folk tradition there are rhythms that repeat and reverberate from the myth and into the practice. Often seekers who engage in útiseta choose to do so in places sacred to the dead: cemeteries, burial mounds, old execution sites, and other places spirits of the dead are found. It is most traditional to do this over three consecutive Thursday nights—for Thursday is Thor's Day, after all. It is important that this be done in the elements—you are not meant to do this in your car, or in a tent. A big part of the experience and initiation is spending time exposed to the spirits. It's said that this practice

---

6   Kvilhaug, *The Seed of Yggdrasill*.

will make one Trollkunning, or skilled in the ways of Nordic folk magic.[7] In this way seiðr is like an earlier version of sitting out, and "to sit" as one root of the practice is a gorgeous example of continuity between ancient Nordic magic and contemporary folk magic.

There's also a deep interest within the practice of seiðr in connecting with the world around you, as in útisetning. The art of seiðr is heavily associated with the Vanir, and with Freyja. She is the one that taught the art of seiðr to Odin. Laguz is considered a feminine rune because of its connection with seiðr. This was a form of magic that was feminine-coded—and Odin's skill with seiðr is evidence that the Allfather himself may have been genderqueer.[8]

Water also has divinatory uses. Whether that is scrying by staring into the glassy surface of a bowl of water, pouring wax into water to read the shapes, or pouring out water in offering to the spirits, water is a great connector to this and other worlds. The suit of Cups in tarot is often deeply associated with intuition, and so when there are a lot of Cups in a reading, it is a sign to learn to work with your intuition. Connecting with water is one way of increasing your own intuitive skills.

Laguz is our psychic sense, our connection. This rune can look like a fishhook, or perhaps an anchor. This rune digs deep into your psychic senses. Through our connection to the unconscious we access inspiration for new artistic work and creative endeavors. This is part of why Laguz is the rune I associate with the moon and lunar cycles. There is an undeniable connection between the moon and the ocean: the moon controls the tides, how that great body of water moves. Laguz represents shifts in our collective unconscious, and how we can make those shifts manifest outside of ourselves.

Rune	Transliteration	International Phonetic Alphabet	Proto-Germanic Name	Meaning
↾	l	/l/	Laguz	water, lake

---

7   Gårdbäck, Trolldom.
8   Jefford Franks, "Óðin: A Queer Tyr?"

ANGLO-SAXON RUNE POEM:

The ocean seems interminable to men,
if they venture on the rolling bark
and the waves of the sea terrify them
and the courser of the deep heed not its bridle.

ICELANDIC RUNE POEM:

Water
eddying stream
and broad geysir
and land of the fish.

NORWEGIAN RUNE POEM:

A waterfall is a River which falls from a mountain-side;
but ornaments are of gold.

Opportunities for Ancestral Discovery

What ocean or big body of water was closest to your ancestors? What associations would they have had with it?

What body of water was closest to you growing up? If possible, visit that body of water and meditate for at least five minutes. Did anything come up for you?

Leave water for your ancestors on your altar.

RADICAL LAGUZ

- Water is one of the most precious resources, and it's also a resource that is in danger. Do a bit of research into the bodies of water that are near you, and see if there are any that are in danger of pollution or other disturbance. If you feel called, find a way to contribute to any environmental groups that may be working to protect it.

- What does water mean to you? What is your favorite way of engaging with water?

- Have you ever traveled by ocean, or spent significant time near an ocean or inland sea? What was your relationship to the ocean at the time?

- Think about how you use water in magic. Is there a way you could expand your water magic?

INGWAZ

Keywords: Yngvi-Frey, sex, portal, protection, creation

Ingwaz is the rune of genetics and the mysteries of gender. Linguistically "*ing*" is not a sound that we often hear at the beginning of a word, and so even the name of this rune is a mystery. It is womb, seed, and an enticing combination of the two. It is the womb and the seed divorced from gender, as wild forces that connect to create life and so much more. I think of this rune as potential. You can look at this as two gyfu runes sitting on top of one another, the pleasure of giving and receiving gifts with people you love.

Many rune workers say that Ingwaz is the "male" counterpart to Berkano. I've seen some rune workers talk about Ingwaz as feminine because they associate it with the womb itself, whereas Berkano is the pregnancy. I like to always think of the energies as masculine and feminine rather than male and female (because men can be feminine and women can be masculine and nonbinary people can present gender however they feel, and agender folks have a totally different take on gender). Ingwaz is nonbinary to me. It has the ability to spiral between polarities of masculine and feminine, to cross boundaries. It's like a constant cycle, spinning in on itself. Diana Paxson associates Ingwaz with castrated shamans and magic workers: they give up a part of their assigned gender in order to gain wisdom.[9] But I think that this transition does another thing: it creates a liminal space of the body, understood as neither male nor female, and we all know that liminal spaces are perfect for working magic.

Of course, the shape of this rune reminds me of a strand of DNA, connecting us through time to our ancestors, as well as to the things that our ancestors pass down to us. The name "Ingwaz" also alludes

---

9   Paxson, *Taking Up the Runes*.

to the saga of the Ynglings, the mythic kings of Sweden. The Ynglings were said to be related to Freyr himself. Their saga goes all the way back to *Ynglingatal*, which is supposed to be dated somewhere around the 9th century. The Ynglings are a very important historic/literary family, and they even show up in Beowulf as the Scylfings. The saga deals with the arrival of the Norse gods to Scandinavia and how Freyr founded the Yngling dynasty in Uppsala.

A lot of our understanding of who Freyr is as a god comes from the Yngling saga, because he doesn't show up as often in the *Poetic Edda*. Today heathens worship Freyr as a god of fertility and agriculture. But I think of Freyr as a bit more feral—after all, we have Thor who also has a great deal to do with agriculture. You can also look at the two of them as working in tandem: Freyr is the god of the land, and Thor is the god of the sky, and when they meet and work together we have fruitful abundance. Of course Freyr has a wife (Gerðr), whose name appears to be related to the Old Norse word for "fencing in." So it is when Freyr marries Gerðr that he becomes lord not just of the wilderness, but also of the enclosed spaces. Thor's wife is named Sif and it is said that her golden hair represents the bounty of wheat in the fields. Then, supreme to all of them, is Jörð—Thor's mother and a giantess whose name literally means "earth."

I'm not relating these relationships that various deities and giants have with one another because I need to reinforce some kind of strange heteronormative marital symmetry. What I'm trying to express is that there is room for so many different forms of gendered collaboration in the myths.

Freyr is a really interesting figure in that he gives up a lot of his power to be with Gerðr. He gives up his sword that will fight on its own and always defeat the enemy. There's a sense of becoming more tame, of giving up some of the more feral and lethal aspects of nature in order to be in right relationship with his bride. This is ultimately what kills him in Ragnarök because he doesn't have the weapon that would have saved him. Even as Gerðr's name appears to mean "enclosed space" or "fenced land"—while Freyr is often thought of as the God of the Wild— she tames him. There's a tension between the wild and the societal. This feels like a tension that queer people feel when shape-shifting between their own communities and spending more time with their families.

There is in fact a regenerative quality to Ingwaz. This makes sense with the Norse concept of ørlog: we inherit the wounds of our ancestors, and it is our job to heal them. If even a small number of our souls are reincarnated ancestors, then of course we can heal these wounds. It may not happen in our lifetime, but this is a big part of spiritual growth. I would argue that for adoptees and queer people with a chosen family, this includes reincarnating within those queer bloodlines—not just your own. We are reincarnating within queer community.

Ingwaz is a wild sexuality that is not constrained to human ideals. One of the things we need to understand as we engage with the runes is that they are the primordial spirit of this force, and therefore they often operate outside of human norms. They also operate beyond the human body—many people who have written about the metaphysical properties of the runes talk about Ingwaz as being specifically masculine sexuality. It is the seed, after all; why wouldn't it be masculine? This is to say nothing of the fact that this is an incredibly reductive understanding of masculinity, but it also limits feminine sexuality to sex for the sake of procreation. I haven't really seen other authors discuss feminine sexuality in quite the same way as people describe masculine sexuality, and the only rune that comes immediately to mind for feminine sexuality is Berkano—in this case related to childbearing.

But sexual energy is distinct from gender—sexual energy is raw and doesn't need to be gendered. And it is incredibly important from a queer perspective to divorce sexuality from childbearing. People who are assigned female at birth have been dismissed for not having sexual desires or drives for far, far too long. To not include feminine people in an understanding of sex for pleasure's sake is a grave oversight.

The sexual acts that are protected by Ingwaz are inextricably linked to pleasure. This is one instance where I think that the many layers of Berkano are misunderstood as well—too often it is reduced again to childbearing and pregnancy. But Berkano is also about healing, and if there's one thing that I have discovered in my life, it is that pleasure is a healing principle. Ingwaz and Berkano are linked, and both are healing runes in a way. These two runes together are about pleasure as a healing element. In her book *Pleasure Activism,* adrienne maree brown put it very well:

> The erotic is a measure between the beginnings of our sense of self and the chaos of our strongest feelings. It is an internal sense of satisfaction to which, once we have experienced it, we know we can aspire. For having experienced the fullness of this depth of feeling and recognizing its power, in honor and self-respect we can require no less of ourselves.[10]

Ingwaz is a primordial sexual force that operates outside of the rules and constrictions we place on ourselves. Whether your sexual "deviance" is the fact that you're queer, or the fact that you're kinky, or that you're not sexual at all—all of that is welcomed by Ingwaz. Any kind of consensual sex here is welcomed. So that is where Ingwaz falls for me. It is a rune of deep sexual desire as well as connected to forces of pleasure, particularly when Ingwaz and Wunjo both come up in a reading about love or romance,

And I say "consensual" sex specifically. You could of course argue that this rune is connected to the sexual act, no matter what. But there is that secondary meaning to Ingwaz that is really important: protection. When the sexual union is overseen by the force of Ingwaz, the boundaries established by Ingwaz are not crossed. This is not something I've read anywhere, but it rings true from my own understanding of the rune and my own working with the rune.

This is the abject joy in sex. It is connecting deeply with your partners and loving them and bringing them pleasure. This is also the joy you feel as a parent, the absolute, breathtaking pleasure of being able to raise a child. I know that it's not always beautiful, and it is certainly not easy, but these moments of joy and love keep you going.

I said at the beginning of this section that I think of Ingwaz as potential. Within the diamond of the rune, there are so many potentials. I love the symbol of the seed for this rune: it's like a lot of potential

---

10   brown, *Pleasure Activism.*

that we can tap, but we don't necessarily know how it will grow. Ingwaz is the potential of so many radical futures we create together. But it is also movement toward those radical futures, because to me it also represents the portal.

Ingwaz allows us to explore alternative realities in safety. If Ingwaz is all about what we create in pleasure, this is also a good rune to use to explore the kinds of things we want to create. It can help us to envision realities that are radically different from our own, places in which there is no war, or perhaps a place where gender doesn't matter. Visualize Ingwaz in a protective circle, and then use the "diamond" in the middle to transport you into this other reality.

You might be familiar with this as a kind of "astral travel," but I'm not just talking about astral travel. Often people travel the astral realm in order to see what's going on in other places, or to meet spirits in a truly liminal space that doesn't have anything to do with your current lived reality. And that is a very important thing for many—but that is not the only way to use a portal. A portal is like falling down the rabbit hole, it is taking you to a different place, allowing you to see things from different angles. I think that Ingwaz makes for a very important rune to incorporate in any kind of ritual where you are meeting other aspects of self, as well as manifestation. It creates a road to get from one place to another.

This is another rune that I associate with the art of seiðr. But where Laguz is the magician working in the psychic realm and the actual act of journeying and divining, Ingwaz is the protection that the magician needs in order to perform these acts. This rune is very good for creating a sort of holy enclosure that the practitioner can work within. It feels a bit more personal than Algiz, but the two runes worked together and chanted together can form a powerful circle for magic working. Ingwaz is also the rune that can protect your divination. It allows you to have a defined space for the different possibilities of the outcome for your reading.

Rune	Transliteration	International Phonetic Alphabet	Proto-Germanic Name	Meaning
◇ ᛜ	ŋ, ng	/ŋ/	Ingwaz	the god Yng or Freyr, portal, sex

ANGLO-SAXON RUNE POEM:

Ing was first seen by men among the East-Danes,
till, followed by his chariot,
he departed eastwards over the waves.
So the Heardingas named the hero.

Opportunities for Ancestral Discovery

Were there any famous leaders in your family? This can even include people who were just famous within your family for the way they led.

Do you have any explicitly queer ancestors? How about trans ancestors?

RADICAL INGWAZ

- What does the image of the seed bring up for you?

- What potential do you have within yourself? How can you work to bring that potential to the surface? For extra guidance on this, pull Ingwaz out of your rune bag, and draw one more rune. Whichever rune shows up is a tool to unlock this potential.

- Free space to journal about anything related to gender—and what it would mean to break apart that binary in your own life.

DAGAZ

Keywords: day, cycles, transformation, integration, midwinter, Midsommar, time, rebirth

Dagaz is the bright, shining day. It is the sunrise. It is generation and interconnection, the true balance of night and day. I love this rune because it reminds me that even in the darkest night, there is light. What's that quote from *Lord of the Rings*? May Dagaz be "a light to you in dark places, when all other lights go out."

Light is incredibly important in the Nordic cultural legacy. Remember: this is a culture that developed out of having two seasons. Winter and summer, darkness and light, and each one reinforcing the barriers of the other. Without winter, summer is meaningless, and without summer, winter is a dreaded slog. Dagaz is a rune of extremes. Other writers have talked about how this rune speaks of cycles, and I absolutely feel that in my own relationship with the rune.

Many rune practitioners read Dagaz as clarity, shining light on a situation that until now the querent couldn't figure out. When this rune comes up, it means that the querent is ready for new information. They have been working hard to understand themselves, and this is the breakthrough. This allows you to see things clearly that perhaps weren't there before. Back in the section on Laguz I talked about útisetning—Dagaz is the daybreak after the third session of sitting out. It is the culmination of the spiritual work that you have been doing.

The structure of Dagaz is another rune that shows us balance. Like Jera, like Ingwaz, there is a symmetry to this rune that is important to consider. There's balance between light and dark, clarification in the balance struck. This is a call to integrate internal and external perceptions, to live in harmony between the two. If you do engage in útiseta and seiðr, Dagaz is a powerful ally in helping you to reach a higher consciousness. This rune can help you understand things at a greater level.

When Dagaz is out of balance, this rune can feel like a strict structure. In our industrialized world we have divided the day equally into hours and minutes and seconds. There are some jobs today where every moment of your work is regulated. This is deeply disturbing to the natural rhythm of our bodies—humans are not machines, as much as we may have developed systems to make ourselves more efficient and make us closer to machines. Dagaz unbalanced is a strict schedule. I've noticed that when I try to add too much structure into my life, my body will rebel. Everyone is different, of course, but I truly believe that there is a point where you have introduced too many rules, too many structures, and it will feel like everything explodes. Your threshold might be higher or lower than mine. Dagaz is here to support us in crafting daily routines that are actually supportive. The brightness eases you away from self-criticism if you aren't able to follow the rituals you set out for yourself.

The Anglo-Saxon rune poem ends the stanza about Dagaz and reminds us that this rune is in service to all. A brightness and a happiness are built into how the runes work; they are meant to be for all of us. The light that Dagaz in particular gives off is a beautiful light that we can all engage with—it is not for any one group over another group.

The light that Dagaz gives off also speaks of powerful visions. I've written in a few of the other rune chapters about how those runes are helpful in divination, but I think that Dagaz is particularly helpful in processing the visions that you receive. Whether you are getting your visions through dreams, through rune readings, augury, or any other form of divination, Dagaz helps you to integrate and understand the messages you receive.

Let's talk a bit more about what I mean by "integration." When I say that I have "integrated" something into my magical practice I mean that that thing is now something that I do often, something that has become an essential aspect of my practice. You can also integrate things into your worldview. As of the writing of this book, I have been working hard to figure out how to integrate the idea that the day begins at sunset. I am such a morning person and have been so fully ingrained in white American culture that it feels really strange to try to shift my worldview to include the day beginning at night. I am attempting to integrate this way of being as an act dedicated to the healing of my ancestors—to return to slower ways. I will know when this is "integrated" into my worldview when the day beginning at night is my first thought, when it is the thing that makes so much sense to me that I couldn't have imagined day beginning any other way.

Dagaz holds infinite wisdom and space for complexity. The shape of the rune is almost like an infinity symbol with pointier edges. It is a loop, one that can be easily carved into wood and stone and bone. The cycle of learning is never-ending. Dagaz comes toward the end of the Futhark in part because it helps us to integrate the lessons we've learned along the way. The rune is used to understand how everything fits together. It is illuminating.

Dagaz is the rune of the opening further into a new world, the knowledge you have acquired through your heathen's journey. Mountfort writes about how Dagaz is the long night of the soul opening into a new day.[11] There are both hope and closure in this rune, balance between extremes, and a new conscious understanding of the world around us. It is rebirth after Ragnarök.

Rune	Transliteration	International Phonetic Alphabet	Proto-Germanic Name	Meaning
ᛞ	d	/d/	Dagaz	daybreak

ANGLO-SAXON RUNE POEM:

Day, the glorious light of the Creator, is sent by the Lord;
it is beloved of men, a source of hope and happiness to rich and poor,
and of service to all.

---

11 Mountfort, *Nordic Runes.*

Opportunities for Ancestral Discovery

One of the most significant Norse poems comes from Sigrdrífumál. "Hail, the Day" is often considered one of the most important canonical prayers. Here is a translation:

> Hail, the day, hail, you sons of day
> Hail, the night, hail, you daughters of night
> With kind eyes look upon us here
> And grant us speed and victory
>
> Hail, the gods, hail, the goddesses
> Hail, Earth Mother, who gives to all
> Wisdom and good speech we ask from you
> And healing hands in this life.

For one full week, when you wake up, go to your altar and recite this prayer. Write down any reflections or realizations that you have.

RADICAL DAGAZ

- How can you think differently about time? Perhaps you can find ways to incorporate more rest in your day, to prioritize this. What would it look like for you to start the day at sundown?

- How do you celebrate big achievements? How will you celebrate finishing this tour of the runes?

- What kind of balance do you need to seek in your life?

- What are your ideas on rebirth? Reincarnation? What does this sort of transformation have in store for you?

OTHILA

Keywords: family, legacy, heritage, ørlog

Family, legacy, heritage. Othila so often represents the very thing we turned to the runes to discover in the first place. For me, when I came to the runes, I wanted to discover the history and heritage of my own kinship. I wanted cultural context for magical practices—I was so worried about stealing or appropriating for other cultures that I finally just said to myself, "Okay then, let's study the runes." I am fortunate enough to have a fairly good relationship with my family, but this can be a loaded issue for many queer people. An important aspect of examining whiteness is to understand our folk cultures—to find something to identify with that isn't "white"—and also not appropriate closed cultures.[12] Whiteness is the thief of culture. As queer people we want to know where we come from, but we are also so very worried that we will not be welcomed by those ancestors and that the deeper we go into our folk practices the more alien we will feel. Here's the thing: we all have queer ancestors, no matter how conservative our immediate or living family. This rune helps us to understand the full picture of our ancestry, and it can help us understand the path that we specifically need to take for healing ancestral trauma.

Othila is connected to the idea of ørlog, which we talked about a lot in the second ætt. Ørlog is what we inherit from our ancestors.[13] These are the threads of our personal ørlog that we are born with. Some might think of ørlog as "fate," but really this is about how our actions ripple through the web of our ancestors. My father has a saying: "You are what you were when." By this he means that we all have a history—and that history shapes us in the present. I like to think of ørlog as an extension

---

12 Takaki, *A Different Mirror.*
13 Smith, *Spinning Wyrd.*

of this idea: you are the result of what your ancestors did in the past, and you have the ability to heal wounds that they bear, as well as make things right that they harmed. If you are adopted into a family, you inherit their ørlog. This happens at any stage—once an oath has been taken that you are now a member of a family, then you inherit that ørlog.[14]

My personal theory is that we also inherit the ørlog of communities we join later. For example, coming out as queer means that you inherit ørlog of the queer community, and especially the queer community where you live. And it also means that you inherit non-blood ancestors who share your particular identities within the queer community. There is already precedence in Norse history for adoptees to inherit the ørlog of their adoptive family, so it makes perfect sense that when a queer heathen comes out, they are "adopted" by the queer community and inherit that ørlog. For me that has meant thinking about the bisexual women who have been cornerstones in queer movements.

Understanding where we come from gives us a new understanding of the paths that are available to us. This rune provides the healing of ørlog recognition: understanding where we might be repeating patterns that are unhealthy in our family lines. This is the deep work of holding up a mirror and gazing into it, recognizing where things hurt and how to do better. It is hard work to be a pattern breaker, but it is critical. Many people who are living out of the closet as queer are already pattern breakers because we aren't repeating certain aspects of heteronormative culture. That being said, I know there's a lot of judgment, internalized homophobia/transphobia, and fear of other queer people within our community. As a bisexual femme I personally have been told to leave queer communities because I posed a perceived threat to people. This was incredibly hurtful, but hurt people hurt people. As queer people we are still capable of carrying on patterns of judgment, fear, and abuse if we aren't actively working against those patterns. This rune can help us to ease that tension by helping us recognize the patterns.

There is great healing that can come from working with ancestors from beyond the grave. Our lives don't stop when we pass away. I

---

14 Tauring, "Frith and Grith."

firmly believe that our spirits continue to develop, and even heal. Dr. Daniel Foor,[15] who is a doctor of psychology and a longtime educator on ancestral healing, talks about the distinction between the "well dead" and the "unwell dead." Basically, there are ancestors who perhaps died quite some time ago, who have worked through a lot of their issues on the other side of the veil. They can be called on to gather unwell ancestors, to protect you, and to work with you. As a disabled writer, I take some issue with the idea of "well" and "unwell," and think of it more as "wise" and "learning" ancestors. In my experience the "wise" ancestors will tend to be those who have been dead for a while, and/or ancestors that led pretty good lives. There are some recently deceased ancestors who are wise though—my grandmother, who only passed away five years ago as of this writing, is a wise ancestor who has made her presence known to many people in our family after her death.

If you fear connecting with ancestors because of your queerness, your witchcraft, or any other reason, know that you don't need to work with your immediate ancestors. When you draw them in, you can ask who they are and what they want to teach you. Once you have made a connection with a wise ancestor, you can ask them for help, advice, and protection. You can tell them the stories of the recent dead who perhaps need healing, and they might be able to assist in the healing process.

The bottom line: You don't have to do this alone.

I do also think it's important to work with the learning ancestors, but you only need to do this when you feel ready and when you have allies on the other side. Part of the reason we do ancestor work is to heal both ourselves and our learning ancestors so that these harmful patterns don't continue. Healing is not always pretty nor is it nice—especially healing from trauma. Sometimes you need to bleed psychically in order to heal. But that is definitely a conversation for later—if you are just beginning to practice ancestor work you should focus on building allies

---

15   Foor, *Ancestral Medicine*.

with wise ancestors. This will hopefully allow you the space that you need to build your own strength.

Now is the time to create an ancestor altar, if you don't have one already. If you do have one, think of ways that you can get more personal with the items you place on the altar. If you know that your great-grandfather was a coffee hound, try keeping some coffee grounds on the altar as an offering. A lot of traditions call for keeping rum or some kind of alcohol on your ancestor altar. However, if a lot of the ancestors that you work with had an issue with alcohol, or if alcoholism runs in your family, that may not be appropriate in your case. It all has to do with your relationship with them and what makes the most sense from that perspective.

There is another term in the world of spirit workers that you might run across: The Mighty Dead. These are spirits of people who were trail-blazers in their lifetimes. The concept originally comes from different parts of spirit work in witchcraft.[16] You can also work with the spirits of those who passed that had particularly fascinating magical careers—I have heard of people working with Isobel Gowdie's spirit, or if you're interested in astrology/astronomy, you could work with Tycho Brahe. Chosen ancestors can really be anyone that you have an affinity with and have something in common with. Some queer Mighty Dead include figures like Oscar Wilde, Marsha P. Johnson, Sylvia Rivera, Christine Jorgensen, Langston Hughes, Sappho, and Harvey Milk.

Othila is unfortunately one of the runes most often appropriated by white supremacists. Because it means family, white supremacists have so little imagination that they believe family only means being related by blood—and of course, if your family is white it is superior. This is a total perversion of the Othila that I know. This has been one of the most healing runes for me to reclaim in my practice. As radicals, it helps us understand what we really want from family. If our blood family isn't accepting, Othila teaches that we can find a new family that works better for us.

---

16   Penczak, *The Mighty Dead.*

"Radical" means to get to the root, to follow things all the way down to the root. In my own work with the runes they have showed me a beautiful way of getting curious and following my instincts down to the weird soil they grow from. Othila has helped me steady myself. It has been a backbone for me, helping me to navigate these complicated relationships. Othila is a comfort, a place where I know I can engage in building relationships even if they are complex. We end the journey through the Futhark here, connecting to our ancestors and the past and finding oneness and wholeness in our complicated beauty.

> "Every way you look at it, creating a good life is the same thing as creating a good death, and subsequently, another good life. Death is the sum total of life."—Kari Tauring, *The Runes: A Deeper Journey*.

Rune	Transliteration	International Phonetic Alphabet	Proto-Germanic Name	Meaning
ᛟ	o	/o(:)/	Othila	heritage, estate, legacy, family

ANGLO-SAXON RUNE POEM:

An estate is very dear to every man,
if he can enjoy there in his house
whatever is right and proper in constant prosperity.

Opportunities for Ancestral Discovery

All of the journaling questions around Othila can honestly be about ancestors. If you've never looked into your ancestors, your homework for the ancestral part of this is to think about what your ancestors mean to you. After all of the work you've done so far in this course, what ancestors do you want to work with? Do you need to do research into your ancestors?

Use this space to brainstorm any of the practicalities of ancestral work.

RADICAL OTHILA

- Write out the threads of ørlog that you're a part of. This can be your family, your chosen family, and instances where you feel like you're a part of a collective. Take your time with this.

- Are there any patterns that you're noticing? Patterns can include: specific kinds of mental illness, traditions, times of year that are joyful or difficult, shared experiences that you don't talk about often (both have had abortions, getting sick at the same time, similar trust issues, and the like.)

- What would it look like to honor these parts of your experience? How can you honor the shadow that your lineage is showing you?

- What are some gifts that come with your ancestors or chosen family community?

- How can you honor and pass along those gifts?

7

Using Runes in Divination

One of the primary reasons that people begin to learn runes, or perhaps encounter them for the first time, is through the use of runes for divination. This is also a very good way of getting to know the runes and their energy as you are getting started working with them. Funny story: This is actually not at all how I started working with the runes. When I was doing coven work as a teen, the high priest and high priestess of the coven were rune workers and did have an emphasis on runes and some Norse magic in their own practices. Of course, this coven was not a heathen coven per se, but a lot of people coming together who largely practiced Wiccan rituals, and others in the coven worked within different pantheons. I do distinctly remember having a three-rune reading pulled for me on several occasions, often when I was attempting to make a decision or figure out where to go next in my magical practice. But when I really started to work with runes, it was because of their magical associations. I dress my own candles for magic, and runes are relatively easy to carve into the wax in order to charge the candle for the working.

However, this haphazard approach to the runes was not really to learn the runes and build a relationship with them. I was really just looking up runes in a correspondence table, and it wasn't until I started working with runes more often for divination that I developed a much deeper relationship with them. This is when I actually felt like I began to get to know them on an energetic level and utilize them in new ways magically. So this is why I advocate so strongly for my students to begin in the opposite direction from what I did. Start with divination, and move your way forward. Pulling a rune a day also helps with memorization—something that is more necessary for complex rune readings and workings.

The runes act like primal energies, and like anything, it's important to build your relationship with them. I find sometimes that my rune readings feel almost like a conversation. They can be cantankerous, lively, rude, mystical, or any number of other things. It's like talking to an ancient being, and you might catch them in one mood or another, but they always have wisdom to share. In this section, I'll cover several ways that you can start to learn divination with runes. We will start with the simplest forms of divination and move forward from there.

One-Rune Readings

This is the "daily rune" or the reading that is focused on just one rune to answer a question. I say that this is a good daily reading because it is simple enough that you can get to know the runes and begin incorporating them into your life. Runes are also fairly easy to carry with you throughout the day, so you can pull a rune in the morning and then keep it in your pocket for the rest of the day. This will help you get to know that particular rune's energy, and if you are able to pay attention and keep it in your mind throughout the day, you might find that there are particular "aha!" moments that can help clarify that rune's meaning for you.

The method for drawing one rune readings is simple. Find a comfortable position and get grounded. Now, reach out energetically and ask what the runes have in store for you for the day. You can also ask about a particular situation or event you have coming up, like "How can I prepare for this meeting?" or "What do I need to know about the event I'm going to tonight?" Then, you will reach your hand into the rune bag and pull out a rune! Take some time, perhaps read some meanings for the rune, and go about your day.

Two-Rune Readings

The most common form of rune pull is either the one-rune reading or the three-rune reading. However, I have always been a fan of two-rune or two-card readings (depending on what divination method I'm using). These can be especially good when you need a bit more detail, but also need the runes to "tell it like it is." Another important aspect of the two-rune reading is the exploration of duality, or polarity. Of course, as a nonbinary rune reader I like to break apart binaries, but sometimes they can be helpful. Think about it more like in astrology: working with the nodes can provide some insight: two opposite signs working together. This is a great reading for when you need to think about two vastly different viewpoints or modes of being.

Here are some sample two-rune questions:

- Energy + Action (the two rune spread I pull the most)

- Summer + Winter

- Self + Collective

- Self + Partner

- Receptive Energy + Active Energy

- Give + Take

This process will look much the same as the process for the first reading, which is to get grounded, and reach into the bag and pull two runes. You can choose to carry them, or write them in your planner for the day, or do whatever will help you keep that energy close at hand.

Three-Rune Readings

Like I explained earlier, the three-rune reading is one of the most common readings. There is something about the number three that is particularly satisfying to occultists of all stripes. Three is a very sacred number in Nordic mythology; it is a numerical motif that appears over and over again. Or rather, threes and multiples of three show up over and over.

There are three Norns, nine worlds, nine healing goddesses, the list goes on and on. Threes are also a very important number in fairy tales and folktales: Goldilocks and the Three Bears, Three Billy Goats Gruff, countless stories with three sisters or three brothers. Furthermore, there is evidence that the three-rune reading was in use as early as Tacitus. Remember Tacitus, and *Germania*? There is a clear description of some form of reading, which I will talk about here.

> They attach the highest importance to the taking of auspices and casting lots. Their usual procedure with the lot is simple. They cut off a branch from a nut-bearing tree and slice it into strips. These they mark with different signs and throw them at random onto a white cloth. Then the state's priest, if it is an official consultation, or the father of the family, in a private one, offers prayer to the gods and looking up towards heaven picks up three strips, one at a time, and, according to which sign they have previously been marked with, makes his interpretation. If the lots forbid an undertaking, there is no deliberation that day about the matter in question. If they allow it, further confirmation is required by taking auspices.[1]

So the method described here is to throw the runes on the cloth, look to the heavens, and pull three runes from what has fallen. Then, you can determine what course of action to take next.

The most common three-rune reading is the Past, Present, and Future reading, but I want to complicate it—or perhaps simplify it?—for you a little bit. The Norse saw time in a very different way, and if we want to get closer to our roots, we can attempt to look at this time-bound reading in a different way. The three-rune reading is often referred to as a "Norn" reading, with each rune getting assigned the qualities of one of the runes.

Urðr represents the past, memory, and that which is. "That which is" sounds like the present, doesn't it? But no, "that which is" represents the things that have already happened, leading up into this present moment.

---

1   Tacitus, *The Agricola and the Germania of Tacitus*.

Actions should be taken based on that which is. This helps to cut down our anxiety. We already know what has happened; we don't need to stress endlessly trying to predict the future or know what others are doing in this moment. Make decisions based on the information you have.

Verðandi is the present moment, the beautiful moment that you are in right now. This is your primary focus for the day. Urðr may provide context for why certain things are happening, or how you got to this current situation, but Verðandi shows where the action truly lies. I know a lot of readers tend to move quickly through the present moment in this kind of spread, but I think it's essential to slow down and think about the present moment. In Norse culture we talk about this as the moment of becoming. This is where you can mold the future, which I think is honestly the reason I ever do a past-present-future spread. This shows the tools to use to create the most favorable outcome.

Skuld is the Norn most often associated with the future. This is the most secretive Norn, and technically the one we will never meet. We can never truly be in the future, and we can never truly know the future. Whenever I pull a rune for outcomes, I think of it as a potentiality. It is a potential outcome; it could happen this way. In this spread, I think of the future rune as the outcome that will come to pass if either (a) you keep going down the path you're on, or (b) you listen to the runes' advice. It is never set in stone; there is always the potential to change your future.

There are two options for performing this reading. First, you can pull three runes from the bag as you have for the other readings so far. Or, if you would like to begin to understand how throwing runes works, you can cast runes on your cloth, look to the sky, and pull three runes from the cloth.

The Rune Cloth

Before I talk about reading a casting of runes, I need to talk about the rune cloth. This is an important tool that I use in rune reading that acts likes the magical container of the rune reading. This is a cloth that I use only to perform readings; it has no other use or magical purpose. Traditionally, the rune cloth is white. It's thought that this is because the rune cloth is a holy object, and it would have been very difficult to keep white in ancient times—so it shows the dedication of the rune reader. I don't know how much truth there is to this claim. I do have a strong preference that my rune cloth be simple, so no patterned fabric or overly prescriptive illustrations. This serves a couple of purposes: it will be easier to see patterns in the runes as they are cast, and it will also be more versatile in the long run. My rune cloth is a yellowish cream with a big gray circle in the middle. When I cast my runes, I will often see many runes that have fallen outside of the gray circle. In my workings, those are runes that pertain to other situations the querent may be facing, or alternatively to issues that are not relevant that the querent doesn't need to worry about. But honestly, whatever cloth you connect with is most important—you are developing a rune practice for yourself.

Another thing that we need to talk about is consecrating rune cloths. There are so many ways that you can do this, and it is deeply personal for you. It is traditional to consecrate a rune set with blood, but I would not apply this to the rune cloth itself. You could leave your cloth out under a full moon. You could light some herbs and run their smoke over the cloth. You could mist the cloth with your favorite magical perfume. As long as you dedicate the action you're taking to consecrating the cloth and do it with gravity, whatever will connect you to the magic of the rune cloth and help you feel centered when you cast the runes is the most important practice.

CASTING ON A RUNE CLOTH

This can be incredibly intimidating! I definitely don't think that you should cast on a rune cloth without having a firm understanding of the runes themselves and working with them on an individual basis first. I would recommend putting in a significant amount of study with the runes before you cast on a cloth, as their energy and interaction with one another as they fall randomly on the cloth can be confusing. I had been practicing with runes for two years before I began casting on a cloth. Once you feel ready, working on a rune cloth will help you to have a greater understanding of the runes and be in a more active conversation with them. When you throw runes, you can see groupings, runes that are drawn to one another, and where they fall in relation to each other. You can see what is present—and sometimes, what isn't. This sort of chaotic reckoning can help you

I have a bit of a process around how I cast runes, and I hope that breaking it down this way for you will help you to feel more secure in reading them.

Develop your question.

Sometimes this is the hardest part of getting a reading! I know that I have many clients who just know they need help, but aren't sure how to articulate the help they need. In this case, I usually ask a few questions for clarity, and if there's anything the client needs to know for their healing. Another way of narrowing things down when you're not sure what question you want to ask is to think about all of the different things happening in your life. Perhaps grab a piece of scratch paper or your journal and free write for a while. The themes that keep coming up are likely the places where you need some clarity. Or perhaps it feels like there's something missing from whatever you've written—and writing it out in your journal can help show you those holes.

If you already have an idea for what you want to gain from the reading, great! Let's talk about refining your question. I like to come to readings with a fairly open-ended question. I usually don't do a full reading on a yes/no question (using a pendulum is perfect for this). And if it's a specific or really focused reading, like questions about how to approach a particular situation, try a three-rune reading first and see what comes up there. However, if there are things about the situation that you don't know about, or that are outside forces, a fully thrown reading might be right for you.

What are some examples of great questions? Here are a few to get you thinking:

- What can I do to find more ease and grace in my life?

- Things are hard with my family right now. What do I need to know before I see people?

- Things are really difficult and I've got a lot of trauma coming up for me. How can I find some healing?

- What would my unconscious like to tell me?

- How can I use my creative energy best right now?

- What can I do to attract love in my life?

Notice that these are open-ended questions, and they also give a little bit of context. I think that it's nice to give a bit of grounding in the situation, because you're essentially asking for guidance on something. I definitely have an animistic relationship with my runes (which means that I see them almost as a collection of spirits that I work with), and so I want to give those spirits a bit of context. This will also help gently guide the runes, while still leaving space for them to have something to say about other aspects of your life.

Figure out what different areas of your rune cloth mean.

There are several different ways that you might want to divide a rune cloth spread, and they will work best for different kinds of questions. I don't have one way that I do it; it's purely dependent on the reading itself and what I think will make the most sense. If you would like to make a cloth division really easy instead of eyeballing it, you can use a fabric chalk or fabric pencil to make your divisions and then simply erase it or wash the cloth and it will be gone. The most important thing is to decide what those divisions are before you throw the runes.

I usually divide the cloth horizontally, so that there is one half in front of me and one half further away. Whatever falls in the top half of the circle is usually something external or outside of myself or my control. Whatever falls closer to myself is a more internal process—stuff I have to do on my own, or perhaps an internal healing process. So for example, if there is something dividing my family and it is hurting my family members, I might have the bottom half of the circle represent my own thoughts, feelings, and actions I should take in the situation, and the top half will be for the other family members who are impacted by the situation, so that I can understand where they're coming from.

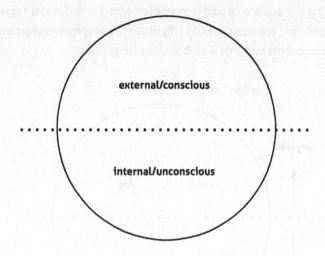

When it's a reading that involves only myself it can be useful to divide the cloth along the lines of "conscious" and "unconscious." Runes that fall in the conscious realm might show me some clarity on the things I already know are impacting me, like not being paid well enough for the work that I do or feeling added stress from an ongoing conflict. The unconscious realm would help me to shine additional light on the situation: those things that I haven't yet been able to articulate in my conscious mind but are having an impact under the surface. This might include hints about what is happening for other people in the conflict, or other things that are influencing my decisions that I didn't think were related. This area of the cloth reveals things about my inner working that I don't consciously understand. Another division, and this could be a horizontal or vertical line, is for the energy and action of a situation. The energy will help you to read what the internal processes are, the energy surrounding a situation, and then the runes that fall in the action part of the circle are the runes that tell you what to do about it.

You can also divide the cloth into four. There are a lot of ways to do this, but I like to think of it as an expansion of dividing the cloth in two. The horizontal line might divide between you and the collective, and then a vertical line might divide between energy and action. You can also make the quadrants of the cloth represent fully separate things. For example, you could ask about trying to find balance in your life by assigning the quadrants to different elements. For me, water represents emotions, fire represents what I fight for, air represents learning, and earth represents material well-being/healing.

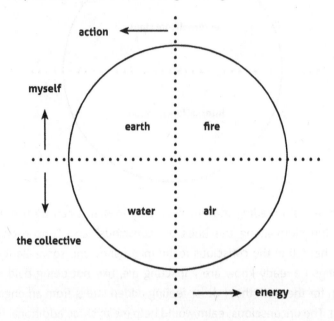

Dividing the cloth into three can help you with an extended Past-Present-Future (Urðr-Verðandi-Skuld) reading. In this division, the section on the left represents the past, the section in the middle represents the present, and the section on the right represents the future. This is great for when you have a question about your own history in a situation and how to move forward. I use this in readings about trauma, love life, creative endeavors, anything. If you feel like the three-rune reading would work, but isn't in-depth enough, this is where you can expand. It is important to recognize here that there is no future tense in Old Norse, so the future here is more about possibility than what is laid in stone. It tells you more about what you are attempting to work toward than what will happen. This is a reading where using the fabric chalk can be really nice because it can be difficult to figure out where the different runes fall on the cloth without a dividing line.

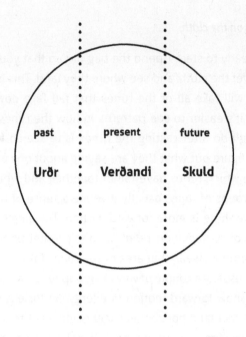

past : present : future

Urðr : Verðandi : Skuld

Another kind of reading that would utilize this cloth division is the mind-body-soul reading. You can use this reading for an in-depth look at different areas of your spiritual health. Mind can represent what's going on for you with mental health, any kinds of things to look out for in that realm. Body can represent some very real bodily issues that may need healing. This will be especially important for people with chronic illnesses or pain, but could also help you understand how to work with your body and treat it better in the moment. Finally, the soul section is like a message from your higher self. If things feel off or you're not sure what's really going on with you, this is where you will focus your energy.

Of course, with dividing the cloth in three, you can still divide it in half horizontally for an even clearer picture of the matter at hand. So if you're looking at the past/present/future of a situation, you can also look at the conscious and unconscious, or personal versus collective forces at work. I typically won't divide the cloth any further than that, just because it gets too complicated and the runes will likely fall outside of the neat dividing lines anyway.

Cast the runes on the cloth.

Now you're ready to start. Upend the bag or cup that you use to store your runes over the cloth, and see where they land. This is totally your choice, but I will take all of the runes that fall face down off of the cloth so that it's easier to see patterns in how the runes have fallen. The first thing I do after casting the runes is to search for groupings of runes and figure out what they are saying about one another. Right away I notice which runes have fallen together, and which runes are loners. The groups of runes usually give me a sense of how energy is moving, where there is more forward motion. The single runes might act as a sort of exclamation point, a "don't forget about this!" that impacts everything else in that area of the rune cloth.

There are usually a couple of ways to group runes: a cluster or a line. The line can show forward motion in energy. So for example, if there are five runes that land horizontally, you might want to read them left to right, as if moving forward in time. If they land vertically, it's almost like all of this energy has piled on top of itself. There is no real hierarchy here. Alternatively, if you have divided the cloth in two and the runes appear to be pointing from one quadrant to the next, they might show a progression of how you're supposed to get to where you need to go.

The clusters can be really interesting. In a cluster there is no real hierarchical sense for the runes, they just work together in harmony. Sometimes clusters will straddle the line between different areas of the cloth, and sometimes they will be really definite. I might mentally draw my lines around clusters as my intuition desires to keep them all together if they cross some of the lines that delineate the different areas of the cloth. With the clusters, I like to think of all the ways the runes could be reinforcing one another. They might also represent a particular aspect of the situation you're facing. For example, let's say you're asking a question about how to handle a situation at work. You've got one cluster of runes showing up in the "collective" area of the cloth, which could indicate multiple people agreeing on one way to solve the issue, or a really strong consensus. Think about some possibilities, and allow your gut to show you.

Another thing to remember: runes are an alphabet, and sometimes they literally spell things out. I have had clients come to me about getting to know their spirit guides, and on two occasions the runes have spelled the name of a dead friend or an ancestor who is looking out for them. So as you look at groupings, don't be afraid to look at what might be literally spelled out in front of you.

Find themes as they run through the runes themselves.

This is another really important and interesting way of working with the runes on a cloth. If I'm doing a reading about travel, and three different runes show up indicating that I need to protect myself, that is something I will take into consideration. Or perhaps I'm throwing or pulling runes about a job interview, and I pull a lot of runes about strength. This could indicate that I am a force to be reckoned with, and that I need to show my strength. It also—depending on what else is in the cast—might indicate that I will need to do plenty of self-care after the interview because I need to gather my strength or I will expend a lot of strength in the search process. You can also look for elements of the runes that repeat. If I were to have both Kaunaz and Nauthiz on the cloth, that would tell me that fire is an important messenger in this situation. If Berkano and Eiwaz are both there, this tells me something about the trees and healing.

Another thing to look for in the collection is what isn't present. For example, say that you are dealing with a situation and feeling very stuck. I might anticipate that Isa would show up in this reading. What happens when Isa doesn't show up? Could that mean that you are placing artificial barriers and the answer is in front of you? This is also something that I do with my tarot practice, and I can often get a lot of information from what isn't in a spread.

Compile and synthesize.

This whole process probably sounds very long! But I'll tell you that it's usually pretty quick for me. I'll make note of the groupings and the other information, and then interpret freely. I'll choose one area of the cloth and move gradually through all of the runes, writing out what I think the groupings and individual runes mean, and what isn't present. After I've sat with the runes as cast for a while, just looking at them, I'll start to write freely. This can sometimes feel like automatic writing for me because it's almost like the messages take over and come through clearly. It might feel more natural for you to talk through the runes and record yourself as you go. That's okay! I will often just whip out my phone and do a voice recording as I talk through the runes.

It takes a while to build up this kind of affinity, so be patient with yourself if you feel overwhelmed. Take a picture of the casting and come back to it. Just don't start another reading with the runes before you've finished synthesizing your thoughts from this one. If you leave the interpretation for too long, you might start to feel a drain on your energy. I definitely recommend finishing the reading within a day of the casting.

Rune Reading Cast upon a Cloth

And now, I wanted to provide you with an example of a rune reading cast upon a cloth. This is a pretty intimidating form of divination if you've never seen one in action, so I wanted to make sure to provide you with this resource; the example is shown on page 185. Making a cloth for casting is pretty simple—this drawing shows a plain fabric onto which I've sewn another circle-shaped piece of fabric. This circle is the reading area. You can also take a plain cloth, such as a plain tea towel or napkin, and draw a circle on it with a marker.

For this reading, I decided to cast some runes that would hopefully be applicable to many of the people reading this book. I wanted to get a reading that would help us understand how to connect with the ørlog of the queer ancestors. I brought myself into a meditative state and began to focus on my question. I wanted to know what kinds of support we will need from our past, that which is becoming, and the choices we make to honor our queer ancestors as we move into the future. I asked for gentle, general advice that would help the greatest number of people. The question came to me as:

"What does a reciprocal relationship with queer ancestors look like? And how can we provide and receive support?"

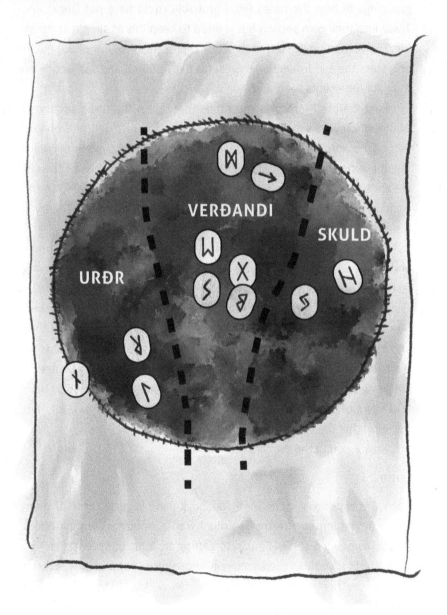

As you can see from the illustration, for the purpose of interpretion, I've divided the cloth into three different sections marked by dashed lines. They aren't straight up-and-down lines but rather based on the groupings of how the runes fell. I probably could have put Dagaz and Tiwaz into their own section but wanted to keep this as simple as possible. The section on the left of the cloth represents the Urðr of our queer ancestors, the middle section represents the Verðandi, and the section on the right represents the Skuld.

First, before I interpret the runes that fell in the three sections I outlined above, I want to interpret Nauthiz, ᚾ, which fell half on and half off the circular reading area. In my own internal system for reading, the runes that fall on the cloth but outside the bounds of the circle are runes that are important but are not necessarily related to the primary question at hand. The only rune that falls into this category is Nauthiz.

I see this as a generally cautionary rune. Focus on what you need, and not necessarily on what you desire. I know this is a reading that will last hopefully through decades, but at the time of writing this book, I feel like there are some troubling things in our path as a queer community. These times have been very unstable for many people, including and especially the queer community. Now is a good time to focus on our baseline, creating a strong foundation and really focusing on needs. I'm going to put this another way: What essentials do you need to have taken care of in order to pave the way toward liberation? This is another question that the runes are inviting you to explore.

Now . . . on to the primary reading.

URÐR

There are two runes in this area: Raidho, ᚱ, and Laguz, ᛚ. Both of them are an invitation into further spiritual work. Sometimes I think about Raidho as being a sort of "guide to getting to know our soul parts." It's a vehicle that you can use to move to those other parts of yourself and get to know them. So here, Raidho is like the vehicle that you can use to travel to the ancestral lands. There are even soul parts that are made up in part by your ancestors! This rune showing up here shows that they are close to us. There is also a sense of travel with this rune, of spirit flight while maintaining your groundedness.

Raidho is also connected here with Laguz, the rune of the lake and the water. This again speaks to the essential nature of travel, but this time over water. Water is the element of healing, but it is also one of relating. It can be a mirror—and in this way, Laguz holds up a mirror to us to see that we are not so different from our queer ancestors. We are not so separated by the years that we cannot recognize one another. The runes are attempting to say that our similarities can teach us more than our differences. If queer ancestors were just like you, how did they get along?

Both of these runes together in this area of the reading speak to both practical ways of connecting with queer ancestors as well as more esoteric ways of connecting with them. Maybe one of the practical ways you can honor them in this life is through traveling to see historic queer places, like the Stonewall Inn in New York City. A more esoteric way might be to take a ritual bath and attempt to connect with them there.

VERÐANDI

I've found that most of my rune castings following this past-present-future or Urðr-Verðandi-Skuld division have most of the runes showing up in this section, and this reading is not any different.

I'll start by interpreting the cluster of four runes: Ehwaz, M, Sowilo, ∫, Berkano, ß, and Gyfu, X. Ehwaz is all about relationships and working together, and so of course it makes sense that it would be in this area! If you are intending to create lasting relationships with queer ancestors, Ehwaz is a great rune to help cultivate that. Sowilo is a rune of success, and here we see that we're shining a light on our relationships. There are plenty of successes happening today, and the queer ancestors are so proud of you/me/us for making it this far and making the strides that we have. Sowilo turns everything to gold, and the way that it's touching Ehwaz here shows that we can turn our relationships to gold.

Next we have Gyfu, a rune of reciprocity and gift giving. This is an important time to perhaps think about the gifts that our queer ancestors gave to us that are still available. For example, you could think of this like the art and music that have been handed down to us, or the philosophies. And we give back by living our full lives. Berkano is resting on top of Gyfu, a show of healing and solidarity. Grow where you are planted, and allow yourself to heal. Remember that your healing is a gift to the ancestors, and they are here to assist us in our own healing—because as we grow, we reach back and heal them.

This cluster together is an incredibly hopeful vision of what queer community can be and is. I hope that it shows up as an affirmation that if you're reading this book, if you're doing the work, then you are well supported.

There are two other runes in this area of the cloth: Dagaz, ᛞ, and Tiwaz, ᛏ. Dagaz is another sunny rune, and because both Dagaz and Sowilo are here we see there is an extra emphasis on the present. I also think that it's not a surprise that this seems to place Tiwaz—justice—at the center of our concerns for the present moment. Working for justice in this world is a fantastic way to honor the queer ancestors. We have a responsibility to take the things we have been left with and work for better. We can do that through utilizing the brilliance of transformation with the direct nature of justice work.

SKULD

And finally, we have Skuld: the debt we owe the past, the debt we owe future generations. It's funny to me that in the above section, it looks like Tiwaz, ᛏ, is pointing toward Skuld. And that is truly the debt we owe: we owe justice to the queer people who are yet to come.

There are two runes, and they mean very different things. We have both Jera, ᛃ (the year, abundance), and Hagalaz, ᚺ (hailstorm, strife). This feels to me like a message to prepare for a future that may not be as friendly, but it is also a reminder that we will survive. We have been through a lot as a queer community, which is something our ancestors can attest to. But we plant the seeds, and we hope for better. Sometimes there is a hailstorm on the way, but sometimes that hailstorm is also intended to break it down. Given the other runes that have shown up here, I think they're offering a choice: learn how to vision for the future, and plant those seeds. Figure out what needs to be torn down, and tear it down. Sometimes we need to make the way for all of that beauty to come through.

8

Bindrunes and Rune Spells

When I was first using the runes in magic it wasn't within a Nordic cultural context. I was using the runes as just another correspondence, like an herb or an oil to dress a candle with. And honestly my magic still worked. Now that I've worked with them longer, this approach isn't what feels most natural when it comes to runes. Yes, you will find runes in your standard books of correspondence, and so the eclectic witch might be tempted to just use them as any other magical material. But there are plenty of rune-specific forms of magic that play better to their strength, and if you think of the runes as a simple correspondence placeholder you will miss out on this deeper magic.

One of the major rewards of working with runes is that they do speak both the language of spellwork and the language of divination. This means that I'll often turn to runes rather than tarot or another form of divination when I am planning spells and need to work something out. It's like this tool is able to do both, which is extremely helpful. But like with any magic, it's helpful to learn your basics and then gradually move up. So we'll be talking about different kinds of rune magic, starting with the basics and gradually getting more complicated. Truly, rune

---

magic could be its own book, so while this chapter will lay the ground-work, you'll need to look for more information elsewhere.

Before we move on, I want to make something about rune magic clear: it requires intent, just like any other kind of magic. And just because the runes can do both divination and magic doesn't mean that they are always doing the two things together. One time in a class I was teaching, a student expressed that it worried them to draw runes because it felt too serious. They were intimidated, afraid of what they would find or what they might set into motion. I wasn't really under-standing them and tried to encourage them that it was totally okay to draw runes daily. Eventually, I realized that they had misunderstood what I meant: they were concerned that drawing runes meant they were casting spells. They were afraid that drawing a rune like Thurisaz might bring more conflict into their life.

But in my experience that's not how it works! And even though I have a serious tone when discussing the runes, and I do believe that they are powerful and not to be taken lightly, I also have never had an issue with pulling a rune in divination resulting in a spell that I have unwittingly set upon the world. For me there still needs to be an intention there—I will more often chant rune names or sing them to call upon their spirits, or carve them into a candle, or write them on a piece of paper and keep that on my altar. But perhaps I'm getting ahead of myself—let's dive in.

There's a large variety of ways that Norse magic workers work with runes, but the primary are through chanting runes, creating bindrunes or rune sticks, and through trance work. There are several different places in the Old Norse literature where we learn about people utiliz-ing runes for magic. I've already pulled heavily from the *Hávamál*, but I haven't talked about the rune stanzas yet. The *Hávamál* is divided into several different parts by academics, but toward the end of the poem Odin references different spells he knows and tells the story of how he discovered the runes. These stanzas are in a different meter from the rest of the poem—galdralag.[2] In stanza 142 of the *Hávamál* Odin recites:

---

2   "Introduction to the Hávamál," in Larrington, *The Poetic Edda.*

142   *The runes you must find and meaningful letters*
       Very great letters,
       Very stiff letters,
       Which the mighty sage coloured
       And the huge Powers made
       And the runemaster of the gods carved out.

                      • • •

144   *Do you know how to carve, do you know how to*
          interpret
       Do you know how to colour, do you know how to question,
       Do you know how to ask, do you know how to sacrifice,
       Do you know how to dispatch, do you know how to
          slaughter?[3]

And after this point Odin lists out several different kinds of spells that he uses the runes to perform, including battle spells; protection spells, spells to dissuade conflict, to be able to discern magic and find witches; and even necromancy. But true to his tricky nature, Odin never reveals exactly how to perform these spells—just that this is the kind of magic that is possible with runes.

The specific verse form that is used to discuss magic in the Eddas and beyond is interesting because it gives us a throughline from possible pre-Christian rune magic on to the present day with trolldom. The most common academic translation of galdralag holds that it comes from galdr (a song) and lag (verse name).[4] These stanzas are known as the Ljóðatal and are written in the wisdom meter of Nordic poetry. They also list eighteen different songs, sometimes referred to as charms, that Odin learned from his wisdom of the runes. It is important to note that the listing of these songs comes after the Rúnatal (stanzas 139–146), which lists different uses for different runes. So what we know then is that galdr has a lot to do with rune magic and is closely tied to Odin. This

---

3   "Hávamál," in Larrington, *The Poetic Edda.*
4   Westcoat, "The Goals of Galdralag."

makes sense, as Odin rides the breath and gave breath to humanity as a part of his contribution to our creation.

Patricia Lafayllve writes in *A Practical Heathen's Guide to Asatru* that these chants are often harsh to the ear. The galdr is a song that is combined in energy with the intention of a charm or spell. Intoning the runes and learning to harness their energy that way is the best way of starting with galdr. The implication from the source materials is that this is a song, or a charm, which is a huge focus that carries through Nordic magic from pre-Christian era up to the charms we know today within trolldom. But more on trolldom later.

A very good way of getting to know the different runes could be intoning the rune over and over. This will help you to raise the energy of the rune up through your meditation and into your working space. It calls in the energy of that rune. The first several times you do this, I highly recommend that you just sit with the energy. What does it feel like? What kind of relationship would you like to be in with this rune? After you have been working with them in this way, you can slowly begin to use them for something. Perhaps there are runes that you associate with the different elements (like Laguz for water, or Jera for earth), and so when you call circle or create other sacred space you use those runes in the casting.

Rune chants are also very easy to do on the go. Say you're going into a particularly difficult situation at work. Head to the bathroom, and chant "Uruz" several times to give you strength. Feel the support of the rune throughout your day. If you're working on a particular affirmation, you can choose several different runes to chant in a stream. For example, for protection I might chant "Eiwaz Algiz" over and over, or for good community I would chant "Algiz Mannaz Ehwaz."

Galdr is a highly personalized form of magic. This is about your relationship with the runes and the symbols that you work with. It's important that you have your own relationships with the runes, and so you can create your own rune songs and chants. In some ways it's a bit of a blessing that we don't know exact galdr because it invites us to create our own songs.

Linguistically, bindrunes show up in runic inscriptions as a combination of letters and sounds. If you end up studying Old Norse and medieval literature, you might see these in runic inscriptions. When they are used this way it is *not* for magical purpose. Again, this is an alphabet; there are many ways of working with them—it is how we use them that makes them magical, that builds that relationship. I use them in my witchcraft all the time.

Bindrunes are a very straightforward form of runic magic. This is when you take the shapes of two or more runes and combine them to create a new shape. Bindrunes are basically a way of working with more than one rune for a desired outcome. This is a lot like sigil magic, if you have a background with sigils. If not, don't worry, I'll cover everything you need to know to create a bindrune here.

First, you will need a clear intention. This can be big or small, but the focus is important. If you know that you need to do some kind of magic, but you aren't sure what you need, you should think about it deeply first. Perhaps you want to draw some runes to help you understand what you're looking for, or you just want to free write in your journal for five minutes to sort through some of your feelings. With any magic, the intention is important, and without a clear sense of what you want to happen, it will be incredibly difficult for you to see good results.

Bindrunes are really a way of focusing that intention into an object, a symbol, that you can easily carve onto something or otherwise carry with you. The most traditional way of creating a bindrune is to choose three runes that you believe will help you in a particular situation, and then find a way of putting them together in a glyph.

For example, if you wanted to create a bindrune for a creative project—let's say a movie about horses—you would choose three runes that relate to that outcome. I would choose Ansuz, to be able to communicate my ideas clearly; Raidho, to help me cut through any red tape and move forward on the project, and Ehwaz, showing a relationship with the subject matter.

Once you have chosen the runes to use in this instance, you will pull them together into a single image. There's no right or wrong way to do this. Some people just draw them on top of each other, some people might draw or carve them as if they are sprouting from the same central point, and still others might just try to draw them as aesthetically as possible. Here is an example of my horse-movie bindrune:

Once you have drawn the bindrune, you will want to charge it. This involves concentrating on the bindrune for a period of time, perhaps chanting the runes over and over again. While you do this, visualize what it will look like when the working has finished. Imagine it feverishly, beautifully; imagine yourself making it happen. While you visualize this, be careful to visualize the path of least resistance, the best outcome in your mind. As you build up this energy into a crescendo, snap your fingers or release it in some other way. Perhaps you want to anoint the bindrune with holy oil, or prick your finger and spill some drops of blood on it to consecrate it.

Staves are more complicated than a simple bindrune. They are a full design, with many different layers. They may incorporate runes in them, but they can also have their own symbology. Staves look a lot like sigils and come from a medieval grimoire style that is a bit later in history.

Staves are significantly newer than other forms of rune magic, dating to the early modern period. Some would even argue that they are not rune magic at all, but their own thing. I definitely see this point, but I'm including them in this chapter because they are essentially more meaning-making symbols and therefore it makes sense to talk about them next to runes. I will admit: staves is an area of magic that I am still learning a lot about. I would be remiss if I skipped talking about them, however. So instead of talking about my own experience with staves, I want to give you a way of understanding them, as well as a bit of a look at the historic staves that we have from the grimoires.

The two most recognizable of the Nordic staves are Ægishjálmur and Vegvísir. These are found in the *Galdrabók*, an Icelandic grimoire.[5] It's important to note that a lot of the staves that we get come from after the Viking period, when Icelanders and Scandinavian magicians were heavily influenced by ceremonial magic that was happening on the European continent. For example, the Huld Manuscript, which was compiled/created in 1860, is the only manuscript that shows an example of Vegvísir. That doesn't mean Vegvísir as a stave is any less important or effective than other symbols that come from earlier time periods. Part of the reason I haven't delved a lot into working with staves in my own practice is that I already have a system of creating sigils and/or bindrunes that works really well for me. There is also power in using these staves because other magicians before you have used them for a similar goal in the past. Much like casting a circle in a specific way when you're working within that tradition, you have support from your magical ancestors.

So, enjoy this exploration of the staves, and let me know how you apply yourself to working with them!

Ægishjálmur

---

5   Lindqvist, *En isländsk svartkonstbok.*

This is one of the most recognizable symbols of Icelandic magic outside of the Futhark runes themselves. Mentions of Ægishjálmur are much older than the current depiction/design that you are used to seeing, and it isn't the only stave with this purpose. It translates roughly to the Helm of Awe or the Helm of Fear and comes in connection with Sigurðr the dragon-slayer.[6] The word shows up in *Fáfnismál*, in the *Poetic Edda*. In the poem the dragon Fafnir attempts to scare the hero Sigurðr away by taunting him with the fear helm.

> *Fafnir spake:*
> *The fear-helm I wore to afright mankind,*
> *While guarding my gold I lay;*
> *Mightier seemed I than any man,*
> *For a fiercer never I found.*
> *Sigurðr spake:*
> *The fear-helm surely no man shields*
> *When he faces a valiant foe;*
> *Oft one finds, when the foe he meets,*
> *That he is not the bravest of all.*

According to Christopher Alan Smith the intent here is clearly that the Helm of Fear is meant to bluff—to make you appear more scary and intimidating than you actually are, and therefore to scare your enemies into an early defeat.[7]

Daniel McCoy, in *The Viking Spirit*, notes that the actual symbol of Ægishjálmur is not necessarily set in stone. Yes, we have this example from the *Galdrabók*, but there are also other Helms of Awe in the *Galdrabók* that you can see. Here we come back to the idea that the intention behind the spellwork is the thing that matters most. The symbols themselves are an externalization of your intention—and then your belief puts your power behind them. Even though runes may have some specific meanings attached to them, and even though

---

6   Smith, *Icelandic Magic*.
7   Smith, *Icelandic Magic*.

specific symbols have meanings attached to them, it is how we create those symbols as one thing that matters the most.

Ægishjálmur is another symbol that has been worn often and publicly by white supremacists, so I would always recommend wearing it subtly or underneath your clothing. It's not the logo of white supremacist groups as far as I know, but you might still get some pushback from community members or unintentionally send up some red flags. All of this being said, Ægishjálmur is also worn by many other people and may not be the flag that something like the Odal rune would be. An alternative to wearing it on your clothes or body is to paint it on the body with oil. Now obviously your mileage may vary, but using an uncrossing or a protection magical oil will give the Ægishjálmur added power.

One of the most beneficial uses for this stave is for protection when you are going into contentious situations. Going into a protest where people are likely to have tempers running high? Wear a Helm of Awe under your clothing for protection; the Helm of Awe will also allow your perspective to be seen more clearly. You will be more likely to experience "victory" at the protest, which would be fantastic. You could also call upon the Helm of Awe when you're going into legal proceedings (though I would perhaps focus more on a bindrune with Tiwaz at the center), or any time you are going into a fight of some sort. It is especially helpful when you are going into an unfair fight, or one where you need to appear more dangerous than you are. Fake it till you make it!

There are other times when you might use Ægishjálmur that aren't explicitly combative. You can also use this stave for general protection and empowerment when going into difficult situations. Say you're going into an important meeting and you want to be taken seriously: the Helm of Awe can definitely help people to take you seriously.

Vegvísir

Vegvísir is a beautiful stave. The name of the stave translates to "that which shows the way," and it is also known as the Viking Compass.[8] This symbol is found only in the Huld Manuscript, which dates from 1860, so it is hardly an "ancient" stave—and calling it the Viking Compass is more of a nickname forged from a cultural connection to Vikings than anything to do with the Viking period.

Symbols don't need to be ancient to be powerful! I usually create all of my own sigils, and I can definitely say that they are powerful even if created one day ago. So don't discount Vegvísir just because it's a comparatively new stave. I think in the case of Vegvísir it has become so ingrained in the zeitgeist that people assume it is much older than it actually is. Icelanders to this day still have a very deep connection with the ocean, as fishing is one of the biggest industries in Iceland. It is an island in the middle of the ocean, suspended between the Atlantic and Arctic oceans. It was founded during the Viking era, and one of the primary cultural understandings of being a Viking is seafaring.

Here is what we know from the manuscript:

> "If this sign is carried, one will never lose one's way in storms or bad weather, even when the way is not known."[9]

---

8   Huld Manuscript.
9   Huld Manuscript.

So take what you will from this particular symbol. I find it to be a guide in difficult times, moving forward even though the way isn't clear, and simultaneously protective. If you would like to work with this symbol, I invite you to visualize it in meditation and learn some of its mysteries that way. Because we don't know as much about this particular symbol, we have a bit of freedom to get to know it on our own terms. This rune has also had its moment in pop culture: Björk famously has a tattoo of it on her arm!

No book about queer Nordic magic would be complete without a discussion of seiðr, because the way this form of magic twists and turns around different gendered expectations is truly incredible. I've already talked about seiðr in other sections and now it is finally the time to dive deeply into this art. The völva is traditionally a woman or AFAB (assigned female at birth) person[10] who is a professional healer and magic worker in the community. I already wrote about this seiðr work as explicitly coded as feminine magic working in the sources that we have; however we also have archaeological evidence of AMAB (assigned male at birth) people being buried as völva. The practice of seiðr involves creating a liminal space for the magic worker to dwell in. There are many ways this is done, and we have several actual examples from the Eddas. Most often, the völva (the magic worker most likely to practice seiðr) is sung or chanted into a state of trance. In my work with Kari Tauring we will also "stav" into a state of trance and from there we will do our own journeywork. Stavving is the practice of rhythmically banging our stav (staff) with a tain (shorter stick). The repetitive drumming with the stav works similarly to playing drums in other trance-work traditions.

Many practitioners believe that there is a womb that is created during seiðr. The womb is a place of primordial soup, the space we are incubated in and the space we return to after death, a place of creation and blood and heart. As a queer person, when I'm reading pagan or metaphysical books that reference wombs it feels like a red flag. TERFs (trans-exclusionary radical feminists) have turned conversation about

---

10   I will be using she/her pronouns to describe the völva throughout this section, but I want you to think of this as feminine gender expansive—rather than exclusive. I already spoke about femininity and seiðr wombs in the Laguz section.

womb magic into an exclusive conversation, one that only AFAB people are allowed. But the seiðr womb is something different because it is specifically utilized by people of all gender identities. It is not a physical body part, but rather a metaphorical one.

And it is too limiting to think of the physical body as the epitome of masculinity or femininity—in their hallmark work on queer theory, Jack Halberstam argues that "masculinity must not and cannot and should not reduce down to the male body and its effects" and the same goes for femininity.[11] Jefford Franks takes this further and applies it to Viking studies:

> By separating masculinity and femininity from the sites of male and female bodies, we can instead interpret more nuanced pictures in which individuals present a mix of masculinity and femininity. Instead of seeing these as binary categories forcing individuals into the oppositional groups of "male" and "female," I instead posit that the "actual sex" of the individual, in this case Óðinn, is irrelevant. Instead the negotiation of masculinity and femininity in his portrayal creates a queered figure.[12]

This wasn't a physical womb that needed to be accessed on a person's body. This is a womb that is called up from the liminal, a womb that would be created expressly for ritual purposes and that contained the völva and kept them safe on their journeying. For a long time it was assumed that only women practiced this form of magic because of the grave findings. The word "völva" was traced back to a woman sorcerer, a vitki as a male sorcerer (some of whom practiced seiðr), and there was also another, stranger bearer of this magic: the seiðberender, the one who walks between, who is neither male nor female.

So here we have this curious instance of a distinctly female-sexed body part being utilized as a metaphor for the liminal work that all of these different kinds of sorcerers can perform. This is a space of deep intuition, a place that allows the völva to see potential possibilities. The

---

11   Halberstam, *Female Masculinity.*
12   Jefford Franks, "Valfoðr, Volur, and Valkyryjur."

seiðr-womb is a vessel that contains the magic worker as well as visions of potential futures.

The womb, in the human body, also holds so many fluids, blood viscera, amniotic fluid—all of this existing in the perfect package. But you don't need to have a physical womb in order to create this liminal space for yourself. That's the beauty of working magic: you are not limited to your physical form in the astral realm. Creating a seiðr-womb is pretty advanced magic, and one that I have felt comfortable undergoing only after years of immersing myself in Nordic folk culture. I don't want to give you an explanation of how to perform this magic because I believe it is best learned very slowly. Again, culture is learned. Heathen elder Patricia Lafayllve said that she tells her seiðr students to learn how to breathe for a year, then come back and learn this art.[13] I would add to that: learn how to be like water, and then return to learn seiðr.

The most famous völva we know of comes from the *Völuspá*, the first poem of the *Poetic Edda*. Odin raises this old wise woman from the dead to get information about the history of the gods, how the nine realms were formed, and she sees the danger of Ragnarök on the horizon. But part of the reason heathens spend so much time analyzing the völva and her role in Nordic society is that we have literary and archaeological evidence that is directly connected to the völva. The clearest description of a völva named Thorbjorg comes from Eirik the Red's Saga.[14] She travels to a farmstead in Iceland and is given gifts and a high seat from which to prophesy. This farmstead has been hard hit by poor hunting and death at the time of her visit. However, she needs women on the farm to sing her the "ward-songs," and from there she can trance and perform seiðr. One of the women (Gudrid) on the farm knows the songs, but she is uncertain about performing them because she is a Christian. When Gudrid expresses this concern to Thorbjorg, she replies: "It could be that you could help the people here by so doing, and you'd be no worse a woman for that. But I expect Thorkel (the farmer) to provide me with what I need."[15] So it is that Gudrid sings the ward-songs and

---

13   Lafayllve, *A Practical Heathen's Guide.*
14   Kunz, "Eirik the Red's Saga."
15   Kunz, "Eirik the Red's Saga," 659.

Thorbjorg is able to see a likely future for the village. She does this through elaborate trance work, which allows her to see the web of wyrd and how the actions taken on the farm will ripple into the future.

This is an invaluable resource to heathens today because this saga outlines not only what the völva needed to perform her magic, but also the high regard in which she was held. Her garb is lovingly described and she is offered a place of honor while she stays with the family. The völva was traveling between different farms to bring her wisdom and services. Wherever the völva is mentioned throughout the Eddas and sagas she is always paid in exchange for her services. Even Odin pays the völva when he resurrects her to prophesy for him in the *Völuspá*.[16] There is a deep precedent in Nordic culture for magic workers to be paid for their services. Considering how essential concepts of reciprocity were for the Norse, it makes sense that the intense energy exchange between the magic worker and the client would be compensated.

Today, different heathen groups are beginning to reinstate the völva as a priestess figure. There are of course differing opinions on what this role should look like. That only makes sense—as we don't have an existing völva manual from pre-Christian times! I am a student of a professional völva, Kari Tauring, and she talks about her role as being the staff-carrier for our community ørlog. This means having a strong inner core and holding other people as they come to terms with the difficult aspects of their own ørlog. Yes, sometimes the völva performs seiðr, but they also hold space for others in the community as any other spiritual leader would. Sometimes the völva will travel to different groups within a region, which can get to be expensive. Considering most organized religions employ a pastor, rabbi, imam, or priest and compensate them financially, of course the völva is paid for their services. The völva is also not only known for divination—but she also performs other services for the community.

Spákona or spámadr or spáberendr are specific magic workers who focus on divination, or are known as seers and prophets. Of course, there is a lot of overlap between a spá worker and a völva, as a völva

---

16 "Völuspá," in Larrington, *The Poetic Edda*.

may be asked to perform rune readings or do other forms of divinatory work but it isn't necessarily their primary service. A spå worker focuses specifically on divination as their primary magical work. A seiðr worker uses ecstatic magic as their primary magical tool, but divination can also be a part of that trance work. The "journey" of trance work can take you between the worlds, traveling in the spirit realm to meet ancestors or spirit guides, see a vision for what healing is needed in the community, and even to understand the workings of the web of wyrd.[17]

Next, let's talk about the trollkunning, or folk magicians. These magic workers come much later in Nordic history than the völva—in fact, trollkunning survived the transition from heathenry to Christianity and continue to practice magic for clients today. Trollkunning often have an independent purpose for practicing magic outside of community ritual. They are not necessarily spiritual leaders—though their relationship to magic is still spiritual, it is more personal. You can learn folk magic without becoming a völva or becoming a spiritual leader in any way. One thing to note about this form of Nordic magic is that it shifted and changed over the centuries. Reconstruction of the völva comes from a very specifically pre-Christian time, but you will find magic throughout Nordic culture post-Christianization.

Trolldom is basically the Swedish word for folk magic, but it is also an entire practice of folk magic from the region. Folk magic shifted and changed based on the needs of the practitioners, and so a lot of trolldom formulas and spells will work with Jesus, Mary, or other Christian themes, and they also will sometimes exhibit dual faithism—i.e., calling on both Jesus and Thor. A trollkunning is someone who has apprenticed and studied under a folk magician and is able to take clients for spellwork. There is a lot of secrecy in the transmission of this form of folk magic. If you are curious and would like to learn more, check out *Trolldom: Spells and Methods of the Nordic Folk Magic Tradition* by Johannes Gårdbäck.

Trolldom is another aspect of Nordic magic that utilizes chanting and poetry, and is in many ways the cultural evolution of Galdr. There

---

17   Smith, *Spinning Wyrd*.

are different poetic forms that you can use and adapt to write your own troll formulas, such as the "as true as . . . " or the "I saw three maidens . . ." version.[18] These are much more beautiful in the original Nordic languages, but if you're not a speaker of the original, you can do other things. I've written troll formulas in iambic pentameter, for example, a form of poetry that is very beautiful in English. Another form of writing a spell in trolldom is the sword letter, which is a poem or cipher written on a piece of paper and then stored somewhere that you need protection.

There are a great many ways that the written and spoken language is used in Nordic magic. Whether you're writing in runes or not, the written word is still a powerful magic conductor.

---

18 Gårdbäck, *Trolldom.*

9

The Continuing Journey

So we come to the end of this book, but it is not the end of the journey. I am so honored that you have traveled with me this far. We have dug deep into the roots of the Norse mystic path, and hopefully you have feasted on a supportive, nourishing practice along the way.

I wrote this book because I knew I had something to say about the Elder Futhark that hadn't already been said—at least, that hadn't already been said all in the same place. There is so much to rune work that is often left out of the popular books. Part of my goal as a queer writer is always to bring new perspectives to the table. Sometimes the only way that I can do that is through revealing things about my very personal relationship with the runes. There are sections of this book that are made up of personal gnosis. I have shared secrets with you, with the permission of the runes themselves.

I wanted to create a book that would allow everyone to study the runes—no matter your sexuality, race, or culture of origin. The runes are a culturally specific practice, but they are not a closed practice. I wanted to provide some context for rune working within a Nordic folk culture— and then I also wanted to queer all of that and blow apart any assumptions we have about gender and sexuality within the runes themselves.

I want to return to a question that I asked at the beginning of the book: Why study the runes?

The runes are a system of knowing that comes from before our contemporary world. They are a language in and of themselves, a language that we can use to connect with nature spirits as well as spirits of the dead. For me, the runes have been a potent way of getting in touch with my own ancestral roots, but they have also been a potent way of visioning for the future. The runes come from a time before "queer" was what it means today.

I had a conversation with a mentor recently where we talked about how, before structures of heteronormativity and patriarchy came into place, before the gender roles became so rigid, "queer" folks were just a part of everyday average life. It wasn't queer then—to our oldest ancestors, all this meant was love and pleasure came in all forms. Of course, this wasn't the case by the time the Elder Futhark showed up, but the runes themselves have helped me see all of these beautiful possibilities.

What is queer when we see queerness as normal as breathing?

Queer is still beautiful. Queer is also still a challenge. As much as it might be as normal as breathing for me, there are still people out there who don't understand what queer is. The queer perspective on rune working is essential for any rune reader because to be queer is to be liminal. It is to live in a space where you straddle the line between different groups. It is also a way of separating yourself from the overculture, which is essential when you are learning any kind of occult art. To queer something means to look at it sideways, to identify all the ways that we make assumptions about a specific thing, and then blow those assumptions out of the water.

The runes being what they are already helps us to do that. I've been thinking a lot about the different divination systems that I use. My first book was about tarot, and I still love using tarot in my everyday life. But the tarot includes images of people, animals, and other things that are associated with our current culture. The runes are deceptively simple—they have their meanings, yes, but they are also abstract symbols. They are at once cultural artifacts and blank slates.

When I need advice about my very modern life, I often turn to tarot. But when I need to figure out something that I can't even put into words,

I'll throw the runes on a cloth. I don't always know what to expect, but it is usually a message that I desperately need. Runes are wild, operating outside of polite society. They will tell you what you knew in your blood, but that you couldn't give words to.

This beautiful tool has helped me understand so much about the world around me; it has helped me connect with spirits and the earth and my animist roots, and it is also so abhorrent to me the way the runes have been co-opted by white supremacists. It is essential that there be new works created by people with diverse perspectives on the runes—too often, the most prolific rune authors have unsavory connections to hate groups, or their understanding has been impacted by these hate groups and it is impossible to separate it from their current work on the runes. I wanted to publish this book to create an alternative source, a reliable source.

After exploring what "queer" means in an occult setting we went through a tour of each of the runes. I provided an essay to give context on the runes, as well as journal prompts for you to get to know them on your own terms. Your exploration of the runes doesn't stop here—it will only grow as you continue to work with them. Whether you pull a single rune at the beginning of your week to understand what's coming, or you add runes to your already existing divination practice, or this is the first divinatory-magical practice you've ever undertaken, the fact that you are carrying on this tradition is important.

And that's really what I want to say. At the end of this book, I hope that you are pulling your runes out and using them. I hope that you are engaging in the practice and finding new dimensions to the runes themselves. I would love for this book to open the floodgates and allow so many more people who were previously intimidated by runes to work with them.

I have learned so much about myself, my family, mythology, and the spirits around me in my own study of the runes. I can't wait to see what secrets they share with you.

Acknowledgments

First of all, I want to thank everyone who has believed in me as a writer, magician, and general human. When I don't have the clarity to see my impact and capabilities you have talked me up so many times. Truly, this book (and my other work) would not exist without you. Chief among you are my parents, who have always believed in me. Mom and Dad, I owe my everything to you. To my spouse Ezra—you have held and supported me through the full process. You have made me laugh when I needed to, and you have shown me so many beautiful parts of yourself in the process.

Kari Tauring: You have taught me so much, and the lessons continue to come through dreams, knitting, dancing, and even more conversations. This book would not even be an ounce as good if it weren't for your spiritual mentorship in völva stav. I also want to thank the broader heathen community in the Twin Cities, especially the Primstav Study Group. You have all taught me so much about this path, and you have helped me to see the nuance and beauty in all of it.

Cassandra Snow: I genuinely don't know what my writing career would be without you. You were the best coauthor I could ask for in *Lessons from the Empress*. You have always been so generous as a colleague, as a friend, as found family. And thank you so much to my writing peers: Jeanna, Meg, Asali, Diana, Christi, Rachael, and Sasha.

I also want to thank all of my friends who kept me sane through the writing of the draft! Max and Hilary—you have always been an amazing support. Our daily group chat reminded me that there were things outside of this book to look forward to and kept things in perspective!

Some of my oldest friends! I also want to thank Stevie, Danny, Markus, Tessa, Em, Jessie, Anastasia, Manny, and Nate—you have no idea how important laughter was to get me through writing this book.

Speaking of family, I want to thank my parents again. This book is dedicated to you, and I hope that in reading it you see echoes of your own unique ideas. I would not be here without you—literally and figuratively! This book would not have been possible without the life that I have had so far and the support that you have granted me every step of the way. I also want to thank my grandmother Ardell Solem. She was my Norwegian grandmother who made us lefse for Christmas, kept the sandbakkels tin in the family, and got me curious about my ancestry. I also would like to thank my Grandpa Barney, who always encouraged me to "get my smarts." My other grandparents, great-aunts and -uncles, cousins, and all of the beloved dead in my family: Thank you. Your support from beyond the grave has been incredible.

I want to thank everyone who has supported me in my business—whether you have participated in my classes, been a patron on Patreon, a divination client, a member of my discord server, or simply followed my writing and shared it with others: thank you so much. I especially want to thank all of the students over the years who have taken my Radical Runes class. One of my students in particular—Z—has grown into a beautiful friend. It is probably your constant astonishment that the workbook for Radical Runes wasn't a real book out in the world and exclamations of "Siri! It should be published by now!" that really got me to actually submit this proposal. I also want to thank my friend Matt—your curiosity and encouragement really helped me get my butt in the chair and get through writing this book. Dominique: Your fierce love and encouragement kept me going even when I was in The Horrors of deadline.

Thank you so much to my team at Weiser Books for taking on this project. It was a special delight to work with you on this book, Kathryn Sky-Peck. Thank you so much for your understanding and support when I needed it. Thank you to the designers who have made this book truly beautiful. You made Lessons from the Empress a source of pure joy and beauty, and this book is no less gorgeous!

Some silly acknowledgments: I would like to thank Spotify for providing me with the soundtrack I needed to write this book. Special shoutouts to Björk, Hozier, Tori Amos, and Florence and the Machine. I would also like to thank the coffee shops in the Twin Cities generally, but especially I want to thank Wesley Andrews, Cream & Amber, and Nina's Coffee for providing inspiring spaces to work when I needed to get out of my own head.

I would also, of course, like to thank all of my readers. The fact that you picked up this book and read all the way to the end means so much to me! You are the real reason I wrote this book! Underneath all of it, I knew that there was something I needed to share about this practice, and I knew that there were people who needed to hear it. So thank you thank you thank you.

Glossary

Aesir: One tribe of Norse gods, headed by Odin (plural form of Ás, meaning god)

Ásatrú: Those who follow the Aesir.

Ásatruar: Someone who follows the Aesir.

Asgard: Home of the Aesir.

Assigned Female at Birth (AFAB): Someone who was determined to be a "girl" at birth, regardless of their own personal gender.

Assigned Male at Birth (AMAB): Someone who was determined to be a "boy" at birth, regardless of their own personal gender.

Axis Mundi: The mythic center of the world. In the case of Norse myth, this is Yggdrasil, the world tree.

Dís/disir: One of the (traditionally) female ancestors who follow you throughout your life. They offer guidance, protection, and support. From a queer perspective the dísir are nurturing spirits, and that is not necessarily associated with the gender of the ancestor who is nurturing you.

Fólkvangr: Known as the people's field, this is the area of Asgard that is under Freyja's control. This is one place you could go after death.

Frith: Peace, the state of mind of not having to defend yourself at all. You are perfectly content. The Frithgard is a place of peace, where no one can harm you and you are protected. It is important to be clear about who is allowed in your Frithgard.

Galdr: Chanting the runes for magical purposes.

Gard: Boundary, enclosure, a specific place (as in Asgard = home of the gods).

Gnosis: A knowledge of spiritual or mystical information.

Grith: Truce, the state of mind of working and collaborating with others who are not necessarily family or your inner circle. This can also be thought of as a negotiated sanctuary. What you allow into your space by invitation only. The Grithgard is sort of like the psychic border between the deepest Frithgard and the Utgard (the wilderness—a place that is not your home or village).

Hamingja: A part of our soul that is related to luck and good fortune. We can add strength to our hamingja through good deeds. This soul part moves on to a family member after we pass to enhance their luck or fortune.

Heathen: An umbrella term to describe pagans who follow the Aesir and the Vanir and uphold other traditions of pre-Christian Norse people.

Huldfolk: The hidden people, elves, sometimes benevolent spirits.

Inngard: The inner circle. This is your home, the people you are closest to, and the relationships between them.

Norns: A class of female beings in Norse mythology who control the fates of gods and humans. They are similar to the Dís, though they are not human.

Ørlog: The fates that we inherit at birth. This can be inherited trauma, unfinished business from your ancestors, and even gifts. Our life is spent understanding and healing our ørlog for future generations.

Ragnarök: The Norse apocalypse, end of the world, the ultimate destruction of the world of the Aesir that brings in the rebirth of the world.

Seiðr: A trance-based magical practice that includes blessings, curses, and prophecy.

Shild: Paying for misdeeds, paying reparations, making things right (linguistically connected to Skyld).

Skyld/Skuld: Norn of the future; that which should be, if you are working toward your best evolution.

Spå: To predict, foretell, to read the signs.

Spådom: The act of Spå; divination.

Troll: A class of magical beings, their sorcery, and magic performed with their aid. If it's in front of a word, it usually means magic.

Trolldom: Scandinavian folk magic.

Trollkunning: A person who is skilled in Scandinavian folk magic.

Urðr: Norn of the past, that which is. She helps us understand where we've come from.

Utgard: The wilderness, a place that is not your home but that you are able to visit and travel to.

Vanir: One tribe of Norse gods. Freyr and Freyja are Vanir and live among the Aesir.

Verðandi: Norn of the present, that which is becoming. She keeps us in the present mind and is incredibly practical.

Völkisch: German ethnic and nationalist philosophy of German superiority over others. This word is incredibly difficult to define in English, and means all of the following things: populist, folk-centered, conservative, traditional, Germanic nationalism, Nazism, and ethno-chauvinism.

Wyrd: Our path or pattern in life, moving forward. We have the ability to change our wyrd, but we are always responding to our ørlog.

Bibliography

Atkin, Nicholas, Michael Biddiss, and Frank Tallett Wiley. "Germany,"
in *The Wiley-Blackwell Dictionary of Modern European History
since 1789*, 307–8. West Sussex, UK: Wiley-Blackwell, 2011.

Bacher, David. "Far North: Photographing the Reindeer-Herding
Laevas Sami." *Places Journal*, October 2012. *doi.
org/10.22269/121017/*.

Baker, Lee. *From Savage to Negro: Anthropology and the Construction
of Race*, 1896-1954. Berkeley and Los Angeles: University of
California Press, 1998.

Barnes, Michael P. "The Transitional Inscriptions." In *Runeninschriften
Als Quellen Interdisziplinärer Forschung*, 451. Berlin, 1998.

Baudrillard, Jean. "Simulacra and Simulation." Ann Arbor: University of
Michigan Press, 1994.

Boemeke, Manfred F., Gerald D. Feldman, and Elisabeth Glaser. *The
Treaty of Versailles: A Reassessment after 75 Years*. Cambridge,
UK: Cambridge University Press, 1998.

Bond, Sarah Emily. "Hold My Mead: A Bibliography for Historians
Hitting Back at White Supremacy." *History from Below* (blog),
September 10, 2017. *sarahemilybond.com*.

Boyer, Corinne. *Under the Witching Tree*. London: Troy Books, 2016.

brown, adrienne maree. *Pleasure Activism: The Politics of Feeling Good.* Chico, CA: AK Press, 2019.

"Bryggens Museum." *Bymuseet. bymuseet.no.*

Burley, Shane. "Rainbow Heathenry: Is a Left-Wing, Multicultural Asatru Possible?" Ritona Books. *abeautifulresistance.org.*

Burley, Shane, and Ryan Smith. "Asatru's Racist Missionary: Stephen McNallen, Defend Europe, and the Weaponization of Folkish Heathery."Ritona Books. *abeautifulresistance.org.*

Burrell, Courtney Marie. "Otto Höfler's Männerbund Theory and Popular Representations of the North." *Themenschwerpunkt: Bilder Des Nordens in Der Populärkultur* (Journal for the Study of Culture, 2020): 228–66.

Burrows, Hannah. "Anonymous Fornaldarsögur, Hervarar Saga Ok Heiðreks." *Skaldic Poetry of the Scandinavian Middle Ages 8* (2017): 367–367.

Cahn, Steven, Stephanie Ross, and Sandra Shapshay, ed. *Aesthetics: A Comprehensive Anthology.* Hoboken, NJ: Wiley Blackwell, 2020.

Campbell, Joseph, and Bill Moyers. *The Power of Myth.* New York: Anchor, 1991.

"Carboplatin-Taxol." National Cancer Institute, March 22, 2023. *cancer.org.*

Cedar Mountain Herb School. "The Magic and Medicine of the Birch Tree." November 25, 2019. *cedarmountainherbs.com* (accessed on 7/14/2021).

Clover, Carol J. "Regardless of Sex: Men, Women, and Power in Early Northern Europe." *Speculum* 68, no. 2: 363–87.

Crawford, Jackson. "The Names of the Runes (Elder Futhark)." YouTube, 2017. *youtube.com.*

Downham, Clare. "Vikings Were Never the Pure-Bred Master Race White Supremacists like to Portray." *The Conversation* (blog), September 28, 2017. *theconversation.com*.

"Elder Futhark." Wikipedia. *en.wikipedia.org*.

Elliott, Ralph Warren Victor. *Runes: An Introduction*. Manchester, UK: Manchester University Press, 1980.

"Factsheet: Soldiers of Odin." *Bridge Initiative*. March 9, 2019. *bridge.georgetown.edu*.

Foor, Daniel. *Ancestral Medicine: Rituals for Personal and Family Healing*. Rochester, VT: Bear and Company Books, 2017.

Gaiman, Neil. *Norse Mythology*. First edition. New York: W. W. Norton & Company, 2017.

Gårdbäck, Johannes Björn. *Trolldom: Spells and Methods of the Norse Folk Magic Tradition*. Forestville, CA: Yronwode Institution for the Preservation and Popularization of Indigenous Ethnomagicology (YIPPIE), 2015.

"German Territorial Losses, Treaty of Versailles, 1919." US Holocaust Memorial Museum online. *encyclopedia.ushmm.org*.

"Germanic Languages." Wikipedia. *en.wikipedia.org*.

"Germanic Peoples." Wikipedia. *en.wikipedia.org*.

Halberstam, Jack. *Female Masculinity*. Durham, NC: Duke University Press, 1998.

Hartsuyker, Linnea. "We Shouldn't Let the Racists Own the Vikings." *historynewsnetwork.org*.

Herteig, Asbjorn E. "The Excavation of Bryggen, Bergen, Norway." In *Recent Archaeological Excavations in Europe*. London: Routledge, 1975.

Hill, Bryan. "Futhark: Mysterious Ancient Runic Alphabet of Northern Europe." *Ancient Origins Reconstructing the Story of Humanity's Past*, August 29, 2019. *www.ancient-origins.net*.

Hine, Phil. *Queerying Occultures*. 1st Edition. Tempe, AZ: The Original Falcon Press, 2023.

Höfig, Verena. "Vinland and White Nationalism." In *From Iceland to the Americas: Vinland and Historical Imagination*, 77–100. Manchester, UK: Manchester University Press, 2019.

Huld Manuscript ÍB 383 4. National Library of Iceland. *handrit.is*.

Izadei, Elahi. "One of Europe's Oldest Trees Is Changing Its Sex." *Washington Post*, November 2, 2015, online edition. *washingtonpost.com*.

Jay, Gregory. "Whiteness Studies and the Multicultural Literature Classroom." *MELUS: Multi-Ethnic Literature of the United States*, 3, no. 2 (June 2005).

Jefford Franks, Eirnin. "Óðinn: A Queer *Týr*? A Study of Óðinn's Function as a Queer Deity in Iron Age Scandinavia." Master's thesis, University of Winchester, 2018.

———. "Valfoðr, Volur, and Valkyryjur: Óðinn as a Queer Deity Mediating the Warrior Halls of Viking Age Scandinavia." *Scandia: Journal of Medieval Studies*, 2019.

Joranger, Terje Mikael Hasle. "The Migration of Tradition: Land Tenure and Culture in the U.S. Upper Mid-West." European Journal of American Studies 3, no. 3 (2008). *journals.openedition.org*.

Jung, Carl. "Wotan." From *Essays on Contemporary Events*. London: Kegan Paul, Trench, Trubner, 1947, 1–16.

Kaplan, Jeffrey. "The Reconstruction of the Ásatrú and Odinist Traditions," in *Magical Religion and Modern Witchcraft*, 198. Albany: State University of New York Press, 1996.

———. "Right-Wing Violence in North America," in *Terror from the Extreme Right*, 60. London: Frank Cass & Co, 1995.

Kaufman, Amy. "The Birth of a National Disgrace: Medievalism and the KKK." *The Public Medievalist* (blog), November 21, 2017. *www.publicmedievalist.com*.

Kellogg, Robert. *The Sagas of Icelanders*. New York: Penguin Classics, 2000.

Kim, Dorothy. "White Supremacists Have Weaponized an Imaginary Viking Past. It's Time to Reclaim the Real History." *Time*, April 15, 2019. *time.com*.

Kohn, Hans. "Romanticism and the Rise of German Nationalism." *The Review of Politics* 12, no. 4 (1950): 443–72.

Kunz, Keneva. "Eirik the Red's Saga." In *The Sagas of Icelanders*, 653–74. New York: Penguin Classics, 2000.

Kvilhaug, Maria. *The Seed of Yggdrasil*. Middletown, DE: The Three Little Sisters, 2020.

Lafayllve, Patricia. *A Practical Heathen's Guide to Asatru*. Woodbury, MN: Llewellyn Worldwide, 2013.

Larrington, Carolyne, trans. *The Poetic Edda*. Oxford, UK: Oxford University Press, 1996.

Larsson, Patrik. "Runes." In *A Companion to Old Norse-Icelandic Literature and Culture*. Malden, MA: Blackwell Publishing Ltd., 2005.

Liberman, Anatoly. "Ten Scandinavian and North English Etymologies." *Alvíssmál* 6 (1996): 98–63.

Lindqvist, Natan. *En isländsk svartkonstbok från 1500-talet* (in Swedish). Uppsala, Sweden: Appelberg, 1921.

Lomuto, Sierra. "Public Medievalism and the Rigor of Anti-Racist Critique." *In the Middle* (blog), April 4, 2019. *inthemedievalmiddle.com*.

Looijenga, Tineke. *Texts and Contexts of the Oldest Runic Inscriptions.* Leiden, Netherlands: Brill, 2003.

Mark, Joshua J. "The Egyptian Afterlife & The Feather of Truth." *World History Encyclopedia. www.worldhistory.org.*

"Maslow's Hierarchy of Needs." Wikipedia. *en.wikipedia.org.*

Matzner, Sebastian. "Queer Theory and Ancient Literature." *Oxford Classical Dictionary,* 2022. *oxfordre.com.*

McCoy, Daniel. *The Viking Spirit: An Introduction to Norse Mythology and Religion.* CreateSpace Independent Publishing Platform, 2016.

Miller, Alfred. "The Primstav Explanations." Self-Published, 2006.

Mountfort, Paul Rhys. *Nordic Runes: Understanding, Casting, and Interpreting the Ancient Viking Oracle.* Rochester, VT: Destiny Books, 2003.

"Need-Fire." In 1911 *Encyclopædia Britannica.* Vol. 19, n.d. Wikisource. *en.wikisource.org.*

"Neo-Völkisch." Southern Poverty Law Center. *splcenter.org.*

Nietzsche, Friedrich. *Thus Spoke Zarathustra.* Penguin Classics Edition. London: Penguin, 2003.

Oates, Shani. *The Hanged God: Odinn Grimnir.* Canada: Anathema Publishing, 2019.

Orchard, Andy. *Dictionary of Norse Myth and Legend.* 2nd ed. London: Weidenfeld and Nicholson, 2022.

Paxson, Diana. *Taking Up the Runes: A Complete Guide to Using Runes in Spells, Rituals, Divination, and Magic.* Newburyport, MA: Weiser Books, 2005.

Penczak, Christopher. *The Mighty Dead: Communing with the Ancestors of Witchcraft.* Salem, NH: Copper Cauldron Publishing, 2013.

Perkins, Camilla, and Theresa Cheung. *Runes for Modern Life: Ancient Divination Cards for Today's Dilemmas.* London: Laurence King Publishing, 2020.

Perry, David. "White Supremacists Love Vikings. But They've Got History All Wrong." *Washington Post,* May 31, 2017. *washingtonpost.com.*

"Queer." *Cambridge English Dictionary Online. dictionary.cambridge.org.*

"Rune Poems." Wikisource. *en.wikisource.org.*

"Runes." Wikipedia. *en.wikipedia.org.*

Salvesen, Helge. "The Historian as Architect of Nations: A Historiographical Analysis of the Norwegian Peasantry as Carrier of National Ideology and Identity in the Medieval and Early Modern Period." In *Peasants, Lords, and State: Comparing Peasant Conditions in Scandinavia and the Eastern Alpine Region, 1000-1750,* 205–18. Leiden, Netherlands: Brill, 2020. *doi.org/10.1163/9789004433458_007.*

Simek, Rudolf, John McKinnell, and Klaus Düwel. *Runes, Magic, and Religion: A Sourcebook* (Studia Medievalia Septentrionalia). Fassbaender Verlag, 2004.

Smith, Christopher Alan. *Icelandic Magic: Aims, Tools, and Techniques of the Icelandic Sorcerers.* First Edition. London, UK: Avalonia Books, 2015.

Smith, Ryan. *Spinning Wyrd: A Journey through the Nordic Mysteries* Woodbury, MN: Llewellyn, 2023.

———. *The Way of Fire and Ice: The Living Tradition of Norse Paganism.* Woodbury, MN: Llewellyn Publications, 2019.

"Sod Roof." Wikipedia. *en.wikipedia.org.*

Sondhaus, Lawrence. "Austria, Prussia, and the German Confederation: The Defense of Central Europe, 1815-1854." In *The Fog of*

Peace and War Planning: Military and Strategic Planning under Uncertainty, 50–74. New York: Routledge, 2006.

Sørenson, Preben M.; Turville-Petre, Joan (transl.). "The Unmanly Man: Concepts of Sexual Defamation in Early Northern Society." *Studies in Northern Civilization.* Translated by Joan Turville-Petre. Denmark: Odense University Press, 1983.

Spurkland, Terje. *Norwegian Runes and Runic Inscriptions.* Woodbridge, UK: Boydell Press, 2005.

Sturluson, Snorri. *The Prose Edda.* London: Orion Publishing, 1995.

"Success Story: Taxol." National Cancer Institute. Accessed July 25, 2023. *dtp.cancer.gov.*

Svendsen, Lea. *Loki and Sigyn: Lessons on Chaos, Laughter, and Loyalty from the Norse Gods.* Woodbury, MN: Llewellyn Worldwide, 2022.

Tacitus. *The Agricola and the Germania of Tacitus.* New York: Penguin Classics, 2009.

Takaki, Ronald. *A Different Mirror: A History of Multicultural America.* First Revised Edition. Boston: Little, Brown, and Company, 2008.

Tauring, Kari. "Frith and Grith: Boundary Setting in Norse Tradition." Course, 2020. *needfire-wellness.teachable.com.*

———. *The Runes: A Deeper Journey.* Self-published, 2015.

———. "Soul Parts and Healing in Norse Tradition." Course, 2021. *needfire-wellness.teachable.com.*

Turville-Petre, E. O. G. *Myth and Religion of the North: The Religion of Ancient Scandinavia.* London: Weidenfeld and Nicolson, 1964.

"Unification of German States—Countries—Office of the Historian." *history.state.gov/countries/federal-government-germany.*

Vesta, Lara Veleda. *Wild Soul Runes: Reawakening the Ancestral Feminine.* Newburyport, MA: Weiser Books, 2021.

Weber, Shannon. "White Supremacy's Old Gods: The Far Right and Neopaganism." *Political Research Associates*, February 1, 2018. *politicalresearch.org.*

Westcoat, Eirik. "The Goals of Galdralag: Identifying the Historical Instances and Uses of the Metre." *Saga-Book, Vol. XL.* London: Viking Society for Northern Research, 2016.

"Younger Futhark." Wikipedia. *en.wikipedia.org.*

Zoëga, Geir. *A Concise Dictionary of Old Icelandic.* Oxford, UK: Benediction Classics, 2010.

About the Author

Siri Vincent Plouff (they/them) is a Nordic witch, rune reader, and tarot reader based on Anishinaabe and Dakota land (aka Minneapolis, MN). They are the coauthor, with Cassandra Snow, of *Lessons from the Empress: A Tarot Workbook for Self-Care and Creative Growth* and also the host behind the radical heathenry podcast, *The Heathen's Journey.* As an unabashedly queer person, they are constantly interrogating runes and Nordic practices through a unique lens of sexual and gender identity. They see witchcraft as a way to break out of expectations and live outside society. Siri teaches about the runes, tarot, and witchcraft. Their signature course is the Radical Runes Course, a six-week deep dive into the runes.

To Our Readers

Weiser Books, an imprint of Red Wheel/Weiser, publishes books across the entire spectrum of occult, esoteric, speculative, and New Age subjects. Our mission is to publish quality books that will make a difference in people's lives without advocating any one particular path or field of study. We value the integrity, originality, and depth of knowledge of our authors.

Our readers are our most important resource, and we appreciate your input, suggestions, and ideas about what you would like to see published.

Visit our website at *www.redwheelweiser.com*, where you can learn about our upcoming books and free downloads, and also find links to sign up for our newsletter and exclusive offers.

You can also contact us at *info@rwwbooks.com* or at

Red Wheel/Weiser, LLC
65 Parker Street, Suite 7
Newburyport, MA 01950